Gender and Culture

Gender and Culture

ANNE PHILLIPS

polity

First published in 2010 by Polity Press

Polity Press
65 Bridge Street
Cambridge CB2 1UR, UK

Polity Press
350 Main Street
Malden, MA 02148, USA

ISBN-13: 978-0-7456-4799-9
ISBN-13: 978-0-7456-4800-2 (paperback)

A catalogue record for this book is available from the British Library.

Typeset in 10.5 on 12 pt Sabon
by Toppan Best-set Premedia Limited
Printed and bound in Great Britain by MPG Books Group Limited, Bodmin, Cornwall

For further information on Polity, visit our website: www.politybooks.com

Contents

Acknowledgements

Most of the chapters in this book were previously published as articles, and reappear here in revised form.

'Multiculturalism, universalism and the claims of democracy' was originally written for the Democracy, Governance and Human Rights programme of the United Nations Research Institute for Social Development (UNRISD), and was published as Programme Paper no. 7 in 2001. A later version was published in Maxine Molyneux and Shahra Razavi (eds.), *Gender Justice, Development, and Rights*, Oxford, Oxford University Press, 2002, pp. 115–38.

'Dilemmas of gender and culture: the judge, the democrat and the political activist' was written for a conference on Minorities within Minorities, held at the University of Nebraska in 2002. A longer version appeared in Avigail Eisenberg and Jeff Spinner-Halev (eds.), *Minorities within Minorities: Equality, Rights and Diversity*, Cambridge, Cambridge University Press, 2005, pp. 113–34.

'What is "culture"?' was written for a conference on Sexual Justice / Cultural Justice held at the University of British Columbia, 2004, and was published in Barbara Arneil, Monique Deveaux, Rita Dhamoon and Avigail Eisenberg (eds.), *Sexual Justice / Cultural Justice*, London and New York, Routledge, 2006, pp. 15–29.

'What's wrong with essentialism?' was written for a conference on Essentialism versus Constructivism held at the University of Copenhagen in 2008, and is published in *Distinktion: Scandinavian Journal of Social Theory*, 2010.

'When culture means gender: issues of cultural defence in the English courts' first appeared, in a longer version, in the *Modern Law Review* 66/4, 2003, pp. 510–31.

'Free to decide for oneself' was written as a contribution to a Festschrift in honour of Carole Pateman, and was published in Daniel O'Neill, Mary Lyndon Shanley and Iris Marion Young (eds.), *The Illusion of Consent*, University Park, Pennsylvania State University Press, 2008, pp. 99–118.

'Consent, autonomy and coercion: forced marriage, public policy and the courts' was written for a conference on 'Multiculturalism, Autonomy and the Law', held in Vienna in 2008. A German-language version is published in Elizabeth Holzleithner, Christa Markom, Ines Roessl and Sabine Strasser (eds.), *Multikulturalismus queer gelesen: Zwangsheirat und gleichgeschlechtliche Ehe in pluralen Gesellschaften*, Frankfurt and New York, Campus, forthcoming, 2010.

I thank the relevant publishers for permission to reprint.

1
Introduction

Twenty years ago, a book titled 'Gender and Culture' might have suggested an exploration of the sex/gender distinction, an analysis of the cultural understandings of gender that get attached to (small) natural differences of sex, and illustration of this via the different understandings of masculinity and femininity in cultures around the globe. It is likely that the unwary reader would have found her expectations confounded. Feminists were already questioning that particular use of the nature/culture distinction, arguing that it falsely represents the body as passive recipient of cultural meanings, and that a seemingly biological distinction between female and male is as socially constructed as a gender distinction between women and men.[1] Those debates continue, though they play only a supporting role in this book. Today, a rather different set of issues attaches to the coupling of gender with culture. Looking at the title, many readers will now anticipate (rightly, as it turns out) a discussion of tensions between feminism and multiculturalism, between the pursuit of gender equality and recognition of cultural diversity.

The notion that gender equality is in conflict with multiculturalism is now a staple of public as well as academic debate. Much of the recent retreat from multiculturalism – especially notable across Europe, and speeding up markedly from the beginning of the century – has invoked the patriarchal treatment of girls and women in minority cultural groups as a key justification for abandoning more inclusive models of multicultural citizenship. Multicultural policies are said to have shored up the authority of socially conservative cultural leaders and sacrificed the rights of women to the preservation of cultures. In the name of equality between cultures, the guardians of conservative gender roles have been provided with public funds and offered an amplified voice on the public stage. Exaggerated notions of cultural sensitivity are said to have paralysed teachers, social workers, even police officers, and encouraged public officials to turn a blind eye to abuses of women and girls. Mistaken notions of cultural respect are said to have silenced criticism of sexually inegalitarian practices.

It is not only feminists who have noticed the opportunism in this, and the implausible blossoming of support for gender equality in societies that find it difficult to deliver even on long-established promises like equal pay. Women tackling problems of violence against women – and particularly those working within minority cultural communities – were among the first to sound the alarm on multiculturalism, noting that respect for cultures too easily became power for cultural spokesmen. Having anticipated the arguments was little consolation, however, when their warnings were turned to such different effect. Much of the feminist criticism had still taken as its background assumption that feminism and multiculturalism were natural allies. Both, after all, spoke for groups marginalized in existing hierarchies of power. Both challenged simplistic associations of equality with sameness, arguing that the pursuit of equality sometimes meant treating people differently rather than the same. Both exposed the complacencies of a formalistic liberalism that seemed to consider the official equality of rights as much as anyone needs. Even Susan Moller Okin, the feminist most commonly cited as considering multiculturalism bad for women, still saw the two projects as 'in some ways, related struggles', because both sought 'the recognition of difference in the context of norms that are universal in theory, but not in practice'. 'What we need to strive toward', she argued in 1999, 'is a form of multiculturalism that gives the issues of gender and other intragroup inequalities their due – that is to say, a multiculturalism that effectively treats all persons as each other's moral equals'.[2]

Okin's modest endorsement of at least some multicultural goals is out of step with current media and political opinion. The problems feminists have identified with the workings of multiculturalism are now more commonly taken as demonstrating the complete incompatibility between the two. American disenchantment with multiculturalism rumbled along all through the so-called 'culture wars', but US multiculturalism was primarily associated with education and matters of curriculum, so the policy consequences of this have been relatively limited. European disenchantment dates from the mid-1990s, when multiculturalism was being blamed (erroneously, on the whole) for failures of economic and social integration, differential employment rates, differential crime rates and high levels of residential segregation between ethnocultural groups. The focus on gender came slightly later, but, by the beginning of the twenty-first century (and mostly predating 9/11), much discussion of multiculturalism had come to revolve around matters of sex and sexuality: girls and women wearing hijab; girls subjected to genital cutting; young people forced into unwanted marriages; young women murdered by family members for behaviour said to offend principles of community honour; the repudiation of homosexuality by leading Muslim clerics.[3] (Repudiation by leading Christian clerics has not, on the whole, been viewed as a multicultural issue.) Multiculturalism is increasingly described as a misguided failure of nerve in liberal democracies that need more confidently to assert their own identities and values. Equality between the sexes is widely cited as one of the boundary-marking values.

In this charged political context, sustained by wars on terror and fears of unstoppable migration, it has been particularly challenging to work through the theoretical and political issues associated with gender and culture. The elevation of gender equality to a defining feature of liberal democracies is to be welcomed, as are more concerted policy interventions (some of them discussed in this book) to tackle matters such as forced marriage or 'honour' crime. But when the rights of women figure as a marker of modern liberal societies – part of what differentiates them from 'traditional', non-Western, illiberal ones – this constructs a stereotypical binary between Western and non-Western values that represents people from ethnocultural minorities as peculiarly resistant to gender equality. Moreover, when violence against minority women becomes a preoccupation in political discourse, this tends to produce merely symbolic actions, like legislation specifically criminalizing female genital mutilation and forced marriage, accompanied by a dearth of serious funding for agencies working on the ground to tackle such problems.[4] Instead of promoting a more defensible multiculturalism that addresses both the hierarchies of culture *and* the hierarchies of gender, the preoccupation with women's rights often ends up justifying more restrictive immigration agendas and feeding stereotypes of minority groups. Real support for minority women remains a low priority.

Feminists hoping to sustain the vision of two related, if often conflicting, projects have pursued a number of strategies to mitigate the starker oppositions. (It has been a somewhat salutary experience in putting this collection together to realize that I dabbled in a variety of them before settling on my preferred combination.) One approach is to identify key principles of gender equality that set the limits to cultural accommodation: certain non-negotiable rights or equalities that must be respected in any pursuit of multicultural citizenship. This is most clearly represented in Susan Okin's work, and has, in my view, been too readily dismissed in some of the contemporary feminist literature.[5] A second approach divides things up according to different jurisdictions, identifying distinct spheres of influence within which different principles will hold sway. This is most fully developed in Ayelet Shachar's work, which argues for a system of 'joint governance' in which states delegate certain regulatory powers to minority groups, but secure at the same time a diversity of alternative jurisdictions. Shachar argues that this forces groups and states alike to compete for the loyalty (one might almost say, custom) of women by offering increasingly favourable gender equality terms.[6] A third approach appeals to democracy and democratic deliberation, with a view to enhancing understanding between cultural groups, identifying areas of common ground, and moving to mutually acceptable accommodations. The specifically feminist aspect is the insistence that such deliberations must involve women equally with men, young alongside old, cultural dissenters as well as cultural conservatives, so as to avoid the 'communities talking to communities' syndrome that tends to empower established – mainly older, usually male – leaders.[7] A fourth approach takes issue with the very notion of 'culture', challenging the reifications that understate diversity and contestation *within* cultures, exaggerate differences *between* cultures, and manufacture deep value dissonance where none such exists.[8] In its interrogation of categories of culture, this has strong affinities with the critique of gender essentialism that became an important part of feminist theorizing in recent decades. It informs much of the argument in the book I published in 2007, *Multiculturalism without Culture*.[9]

A key theme running through this volume is that debate about tensions between gender equality and cultural diversity has been marred by misleading stereotypes of culture, and that an exaggerated language of cultural difference has lent itself to ethnic reductionism, cultural stereotyping and a hierarchy of 'traditional' and 'modern'. In this process, the really important issues have often been sidelined. Cultures have been misdescribed as organized around static defining values; misrepresented as more distinct from one another than they really are; and wrongly conceptualized as 'things' that determine the actions and attitudes of their members. This last has been especially important to my argument, for I have sought to drive a wedge between two very different understandings of culture. It seems unexceptional to say that each of us is shaped by the norms and conventions of our cultures (I use the plural here, because most of us participate in a number of cultural arenas, including the smaller sub-cultures associated with our neighbourhoods or places of work). It seems unexceptional and important to say that our ways of acting and thinking often have a cultural specificity of which we are unaware. But this is not to be confused with saying that the things we do or think are practices or traditions of 'our culture', as if, to adopt Lila Abu-Lughod's evocative phrase, we were simply 'robots programmed with "cultural" rules'.[10]

I have come to be deeply sceptical of the uses of the terms 'cultural practice' and 'cultural tradition', and the tendency to apply these exclusively to people from minority or non-Western cultural groups. Those associated with majority groups are rarely thought of as having cultural practices and traditions. They might, at most, be *influenced* by their social location, or *affected* by their society's traditions, but society is, by implication, more open and flexible than culture, and 'social' influences are rarely thought to undermine the capacity for independent action or thought.[11] As currently deployed, the language of cultural practice and tradition contains within it a hierarchy of cultures. It also tends towards cultural determinism. Describing something as a cultural practice misrepresents what is frequently a contested activity as if it were slavishly followed by all those associated with particular cultural groups. I find myself particularly irritated when forced marriage, which is regarded with horror by most parents from the communities that supposedly practise it, is described as a 'cultural practice'.

In *Multiculturalism without Culture*, I argue the importance of recognizing cultural specificity and context (if you did not think this mattered, there would be no reason for multiculturalism at all), but against the reification of culture as catch-all explanation of what individuals from minority or non-Western groups do. I draw on established feminist arguments about recognizing women as agents not victims, and apply these to the multiculturalism debates. This delivers what I describe at one point as both more multiculturalism and less: more, in insisting on the validity of the diverse choices individuals make about their lives and rejecting many social policies that seek to protect women for their own good; less, in resisting the corporatist claims sometimes made in the name of multiculturalism and opposing policies that cede authority to the self-proclaimed leaders of cultural groups.

PS
143 → See Clodia Kukathas →
Is Feminism Bad for Multiculturalism?

6   *Gender and Culture*

One obvious question is whether this – or any of the other approaches noted above – is more than an attempt to square the circle. Do attempts to sustain a vision of related if conflicting projects offer more than a pretence of resolution? Do they just offer the pretence that we can moderate incompatible claims by declaring certain rights non-negotiable or arranging a division of responsibilities between distinct jurisdictions? Is there a naïvety here that fantasizes well-intentioned and restrained representatives of multiple communities coming together in dialogue and either discovering their mutually acceptable ground or agreeing to disagree? Perhaps most self-deceiving of all, is there a notion that re-describing deep value conflicts as not nearly so fundamental somehow makes them disappear? Why not just accept what critics – and some defenders[12] – of multiculturalism have argued: that there is a choice to be made here, and that we cannot have it both ways?

As regards my own position on these issues, I think there are three important worries or objections. The first is that I exaggerate the extent of cultural essentialism in current discourses of multiculturalism. Who exactly is it that conjures up false and misleading images of cultures as things? Does anyone really say this? Who or what is the object of this critique? The second worry is that I do not leave myself enough of a basis in notions of cultural difference or cultural specificity to justify even a minimal multiculturalism, and that my critique of culture, cultural community and cultural group then forces me in a resolutely individualist direction. This individualism seems at odds with arguments I have pursued elsewhere in respect of political representation, where I have supported measures to address group exclusions on grounds of gender, ethnicity and race.[13] How do I deal with this seeming inconsistency? The third worry is that the emphasis on agency leads me to understate the cultural and other pressures operating on women, and thereby understate the need for policies that protect women from cultural oppression. These are all serious questions, and the last two, in particular, continue to cause me concern. Though it is somewhat back-to-front to respond to criticisms before readers have had the chance to try out the arguments, I want to take this opportunity to address them.

'Culture' and culturalism

James Tully was criticizing what he called the billiard-ball conception of culture from the mid-1990s onwards, and drawing on developments in anthropology to inform a more fluid understanding.[14] Will Kymlicka, probably the most influential theorist of multiculturalism, makes a distinction between 'culture' and 'cultural community' from his earliest writings; he seeks to sustain communities, not cultures, through policies of multicultural citizenship, with a view to providing individuals with the social and moral resources that will enable them, among other things, to question and change a culture's practices and beliefs.[15] Susan Moller Okin, often criticized for failing to register the intense internal contestation that takes place within what she misrepresents as oppressive monoliths, might more fairly be said to argue the opposite, for much of her argument is directed at the self-proclaimed cultural leaders who falsely claim to speak for an entire group.[16] Theorists of multiculturalism now routinely pay their respects to the idea that cultures are plural, fluid and overlap with other cultures. So who are the dangerous essentialists whose rigid and reified understandings of culture have generated a false opposition between respecting cultural diversity and ensuring women's rights? Where is the supposed essentialism? What exactly is my problem?

In a recent public lecture, Kymlicka suggested that my main target is a pervasive but amorphous daily discourse of cultural difference, and argued that it is inappropriate to represent multicultural theory as carrying any responsibility for this.[17] That is, indeed, part of my target, for daily discourse, refracted through the media, has a significant impact on politicians preoccupied with their chances of re-election, and almost certainly more impact than academic writing. I do not accept, however, that multicultural theory can be absolved from any role in sustaining that discourse. First, it is determinism, rather than essentialism, that mainly preoccupies me, for, even when theorists explicitly reject the idea of cultures as separate, bounded or internally uniform, they still tend to represent minority or non-Western culture as more determining of behaviour and beliefs than the relatively amorphous 'society' that is permitted to shape behaviour and beliefs elsewhere. The theoretical case for multicultural policies rests on the significance culture assumes in people's lives, which makes it more likely to exaggerate than minimize that significance, and more likely to favour the determinist than voluntarist end of the spectrum. Arguments, for example, for exempting members of particular cultural groups from requirements said to impose an unfair burden on them tend to stress the great difficulty (moral, emotional or social) that culturally embedded individuals experience in conforming to certain laws, a difficulty that, in Bhikhu Parekh's phrase, can add up almost to a 'cultural inability'.[18] The strength of the case seems to depend on representing cultures as what Gerd Baumann calls 'imprisoning cocoons'.[19] It also suggests a distinction between those who are deeply embedded in their cultures and those (from majority or Western groups) who can wear their culture more lightly.

As regards the essentialism, moreover, we should not understate the tendency to acknowledge a criticism, insert a qualification and then carry on as before. This has been a frequent experience in relation to gender. Hardly anyone now goes public with claims about gender being irrelevant to social or political analysis, yet incorporating the insights of gender into that analysis has proved more elusive. As regards culture, acknowledging fluidity and internal fragmentation is often a prelude to claims about cultural practices or traditions that threaten to reinstate a more holistic understanding. In *Multiculturalism: A Civic Idea*, for example, Tariq Modood argues strongly for an anti-essentialist understanding of multiculturalism, and employs a Wittgensteinian notion of family resemblances to capture the layers and forms of multiplicity that characterize any single group.[20] But he continues to think that 'accommodation and recognition are what multiculturalism is about',[21] and while his anti-essentialism makes him wary of corporatist forms of recognition that promote more univocal representations of 'a' culture, he is unwilling to repudiate these entirely.

Rainer Baubock has recently distinguished between (1) psychological, (2) sociological and (3) normative culturalism:

> (1) a stereotypical expectation of attitudes and behaviours that are seen to characterize all individual members of cultural groups, (2) a conception of cultural groups as clearly bounded and stable entities, and (3) a justification for group-differentiated rights and public policies that derives these from the value of cultural membership for individuals or the value of cultural diversity for the wider society.[22]

The first, as he notes, is the main target of my critique. This kind of culturalism will indeed be repudiated by theorists of multiculturalism, but my argument is that multicultural theory still gives it unwitting support when it embraces one or both of the other two. Modood, I would say, repudiates culturalism (1) and (2), but embraces (3). Avishai Margalit and Joseph Raz repudiate (1) but embrace (2) and (3), at least for what they describe as 'encompassing' groups, those where all members of the group are said to share the same interest in its prosperity and survival.[23] I do not think the case has yet been made for cultural essentialism having disappeared from the canon.

Individuals and groups

Tariq Modood also argues, in some ways more forcibly than I do, that we can dispense with notions of culture; but he considers multiculturalism impossible without a concept of group.[24] If there are no inequalities between groups, what then is the problem to which multiculturalism is the answer? And if concerns about gender equality mean we must resist any multiculturalism that threatens to distribute power to cultural *groups*, what kind of multiculturalism is left?

These issues mirror those long discussed in relation to gender, and, more specifically, to the possibilities of representing women or gender in political life. Cycles of disadvantage and exclusion continue to revolve around real or presumed group difference, and we cannot, in my view, hope to address such inequalities by wishing difference away. In societies where inequality is structured around group characteristics, it is a false individualism to refuse to acknowledge the social significance of groups. The systematic inequalities between cultural groups provide the main justification for multiculturalism, and the language of cultural groups is then (as Modood suggests) an indispensable component in any theory of multiculturalism. Groups, however, are not just products of unequal power relations. They are also capable of coercion. They pretend to or construct a unity where none such exists; they claim to speak in the name of all when they only represent some; they set constraints on those they deem their members and require them to conform to what are said to be group norms. In dealing with these aspects of groups, it is the individual and the rights of that individual that have to come to the fore.

In previous work on political representation, I have supported measures such as gender quotas to raise the proportion of women elected, arguing that this helps redress discrimination practised against women on the grounds of their real – and more often just presumed – group characteristics.[25] I argue that such measures bring previously excluded experiences and perspectives into the decision-making arena; and that the inclusion of individuals from marginalized groups makes it more likely (though it cannot guarantee) that their concerns will be vigorously addressed. In these arguments, however, I have sought to distance myself from the notion of 'group representation'. I do not think we can coherently talk of 'a' women's interest, and, even if we could, I do not see any obvious institutional mechanisms that could link women 'representatives' to a constituency of women. The only plausible mechanism would be separate electoral lists for women and men, or seats in an assembly specifically reserved for women. Though some version of this exists in the village pan-chayats in India, this is too essentialist for most people's taste.

My resolution as regards the representation of women in politics is to stress the distinction between representing 'a group' – which can only be said to happen if the group has indeed constituted itself as such and actively chosen its representatives – and representing those deemed by themselves and others to constitute members of that group. The first involves a corporatist representation where individuals serve as authorized representatives and are regarded as the group's authentic voice; but in the case of women and culture alike, this commits us to what I consider an overly solid understanding of the group. The second – better described as group-specific representation rather than group representation – is a looser measure (in some ways, therefore, less satisfying) that increases the representation of people who share the markers and experiences of the group. I endorse the second, but not the first.

The parallel in relation to cultural groups might be a distinction between respect for culturally diverse individuals (which I endorse) and recognition of things called cultures (which I do not). In saying this, I do not claim that the individual is or should be the exclusive unit of analysis. Individual rights are mostly defended and secured through collective action; respect for individuals includes respect for their collective as well as individual identities, and should involve respect for differences rather than an expectation that everyone become the same. But when a requirement of equal respect is trans-lated into the language of recognition, this highlights the culture or cultural group as that which ought to be recognized. Recognition directs us to spokespeople, pressure groups, community and religious leaders, to the institutional structures that have come into existence in order to 'recognize' or 'represent' an identity group. It tends in the process to enhance the regulatory authority of groups over those deemed to be their members. Respect for people's cultural or religious identities is one thing. *Recognition* of those identities draws us towards something more institutional, and considerably more troub-ling to gender equality.

Agency and complacency

Many of the chapters in this volume insist on the importance of recognizing women as agents, not as captives of culture, and explore

the implications of this for the dilemmas of multiculturalism. The guiding principle is that we should respect the diverse choices people make about their lives, not assume that these are forced on them by oppressive and patriarchal cultures, and not leap prematurely into protective mode. I make a distinction between the policies appropriate for children, who do need protection, and those appropriate for adults, who often need considerably more than they currently get in the form of material and practical support, but should normally be assumed to know their own minds. (I am conscious of the gap in my argument as regards when a child becomes an adult – this is not an easy matter to determine.) The danger is that an emphasis on agency leads to complacency, and that, in my determination not to represent women as victims, I understate the cultural and other pressures operating on them and the sometimes urgent need for (even paternalistic) protection.

I see it as one of the dilemmas of feminism that its social analysis tends towards a version of adaptive preferences, while its political analysis usually commits it to a belief in women's agency. It has become a guiding principle, especially in contemporary feminism, that we should reject the god's eye view that discerns a false consciousness in those who accommodate themselves to what others perceive as indefensible. We should recognize that what looks to an outsider like submission is sometimes better understood as empowerment, and acknowledge that everyone has agency, even though some clearly have more options than others. We should, in other words, recognize the agency of women even under conditions of severe oppression and exploitation, and not ignore the choices they make as if these were no more than reflections of their limited room for manoeuvre.

Yet gender relations – whether one theorizes these in terms of learning gender roles or being regulated by gender identities or performing gender scripts – involve constraints: this, after all, is why feminism came into existence. There is ample evidence, moreover, that people tend to adapt themselves to constrained and unsatisfactory circumstances, and that there is a strongly gendered component to this. Amartya Sen's telling illustration draws on the Commission of Enquiry into the Great Bengal Famine of 1943, when 45.6 per cent of widowers described their health as either poor or indifferent, but only 2.5 per cent of widows described themselves as suffering ill health, and none described their health as indifferent.[26] Given the strong probability that widows would have enjoyed a lesser share of social resources than widowers, this suggests a high level of adaptation among the women to what they perceived as a norm. Add to this what most of us will recognize from a more commonplace personal experience, the phenomenon of coming to consider unacceptable something you had previously regarded as quite standard. Our judgements on whether something is good, bad or indifferent are framed by what we believe open to transformation and what we consider a fact of life. And if people do adapt their preferences to what they conceive as possible, then those with the least opportunities and facing the most constraints may sometimes be the ones to describe themselves as the most satisfied.

If the adaptation is entirely successful, and people are unequivocally happy with their lot, there is something both philosophically and politically odd in refusing to accept their self-description. But, in most cases, there will be some sense of resignation or ambivalence, and often various changes of mind. If a woman says she was prevented from doing something (getting an education, getting a job, leaving the house, speaking in a meeting) but that she realized with hindsight it was all for the best, we do not, I think, have to conclude that the problem disappears just because she has had second thoughts. Nor do we have to assume that her situation became objectively worse if, at some later stage, she finds it unacceptable. If she has adapted herself more or less to her circumstances, this probably means she will not be joining her local women's group, but is not a reason for the group to abandon its campaign for equal rights. If gender regimes had no consequences for the way we perceived our lives – if we never found ourselves performing the same gender scripts, or never internalized norms of femininity and masculinity – gender would be no great issue and feminism not such a pressing need. It is partly because gender does have pervasive effects, on thoughts as well as actions, that feminism came into existence.

Recognizing agency in others as well as in yourself is an essential component in feminist politics, but extravagant claims about agency can still generate complacency. They could, for example, lead one to claim something as consensual so long as those involved do not persist in their opposition or try actively to escape. As some of the later chapters in the volume argue, this could lead to an overly narrow definition of forced marriage as only those marriages conducted under direct threat to life. Extravagant claims about agency could also mean one dismisses too readily policies designed to protect the vulnerable. This last worry comes up most directly for me in relation to a policy of protecting young people from coercion into marriage by preventing them from getting married at all. A number of countries, including the UK, have raised the minimum age at which people can sponsor the entry of a spouse from outside the European Union, and the minimum age of these spouses, with a view to making it harder for parents to coerce young people into marriages with overseas partners. The target is marriages involving spouses from Turkey or Morocco or Bangladesh or Pakistan, though, in order to avoid claims about race discrimination, the legislation is normally framed by reference to countries outside the EU or Nordic countries. (In the case of Denmark, where the entry age was set at twenty-four, this caused much heartache for people whose partners came from Canada and the USA.)

I am critical of these policies. I see them as discriminatory, for they mean you can marry and live with a partner from the EU from the age of sixteen or eighteen (depending on national legislation), but not, for several more years, with a partner from outside. I also see them as infantilizing young people from minority cultural groups, representing them as more in need of protection and less capable of agency than young people from majority cultural groups. There is, moreover, evidence that raising the minimum entry age does not stop families forcing early marriage, but means the young people may remain overseas, with their unwanted spouses, and away from their schools, colleges or usual support networks, until they reach the age for return. The policies can therefore be seriously counter-productive, generating even worse harm. But it is true, of course, that people do mostly become more able to resist parental and family pressure as they get older; and it is statistically the case that marriages involving partners from countries outside Europe throw up more known cases of forced marriage than those involving partners from inside. While I remain convinced that raising the minimum entry age for partners to twenty-one (as is now the case for the UK) or twenty-four (as is the case for Denmark) is an indefensible form of discrimination, I have become less sure about my opposition to an earlier UK regulation that raised it to eighteen. Extravagant claims about agency *can* generate complacency, and the balance is one that needs repeated calibration.

The chapters that follow were written over a period of eight years, thus both preceding and following *Multiculturalism without Culture*. I have edited them to remove repetitions, updated some of the policy material, and added some later references, but mostly resisted the temptation to restate the arguments and make them all internally consistent. The scepticism about culture is a theme throughout, though it becomes stronger and more fully articulated in some of the later chapters. In 'Multiculturalism, universalism and the claims of democracy' and 'Dilemmas of gender and culture', I am still working my way towards my current analysis, but, apart from some ways of talking about cultural practice that I would now avoid, there is nothing in them I would wish to repudiate.

'Multiculturalism, universalism and the claims of democracy' deals with the question of 'outsider' critique. Is there a cultural imperialism in universal discourses of human rights, and is it legitimate for out-siders to criticize practices internal to societies they may not fully understand? I reject cultural relativism, partly because of the implied reification of culture, stress the importance of democracy in resolving tensions between cultural claims and universal rights, but also note the limits of democracy, and the necessity for some basic guiding principles to identify practices most at odds with gender equality. (This is the point at which I come closest to Susan Moller Okin's resolution via non-negotiable principles.) 'Dilemmas of gender and culture' picks up on a theme that is only hinted at in the first chapter, arguing that many of the problems in the feminism versus multicul-turalism debates are contextual, and that the notion of deep value disagreement is much exaggerated. The main problem, often, is how to formulate strong policies for gender equality that do not feed into cultural stereotypes, and how to reframe discourses of sex equality so as to detach them from projects of cultural or racial superiority. I argue that many of the problems are best understood from the perspective of the political activist, rather than that of the judge or deliberative democrat.

By the time I wrote 'What is "culture"?', I had a clearer sense of the exaggerated presumptions of cultural difference that characterize much of the literature and practice of multiculturalism, and the para-doxical way in which a well-intentioned multiculturalism can rein-force cultural stereotypes. This chapter informed more directly the arguments later published in *Multiculturalism without Culture*, though, because of that, I have edited it down quite considerably. 'What's wrong with essentialism?' is a new chapter, which seeks to pin down more precisely what I regard as problematic in gender and cultural essentialism: where something we might consider valid gen-eralization ends and something termed essentialism begins.

The last three chapters turn to areas of tension in legal cases and policy interventions in the UK. 'When culture means gender' draws on material from legal cases in England and Wales where culture has been cited in part defence during a criminal prosecution. I argue that cultural arguments become available to female defendants mainly when they conform to stereotypical images of the subservient non-Western wife. I also argue that they prove most effective, for male and female defendants alike, when they resonate with mainstream conventions, such as the notion that it is normal for men to react violently when their partners have an affair. This chapter is then part of the evolving argument about an 'over-culturation' that character-izes much of the discourse around multiculturalism. Some of it was reproduced in chapter 3 of *Multiculturalism without Culture*.

'Free to decide for oneself' focuses on consent, linking Carole Pate-man's critique of the marriage contract with the issue of forced mar-riage. The question it addresses is how to ensure people are protected against coercion without treating them as brainwashed products of their culture in need of state protection. I draw on Pateman's work as a non-paternalist way of thinking about this. 'Consent, autonomy and coercion' continues with the example of forced marriage, focus-ing on the ways in which the courts have addressed this question. One of the paradoxes is that the more sensitive legal judgments have been those that take cultural considerations into account, but then, precisely because of this, are open to cultural stereotyping. The volume as a whole is concerned with how to register the significance of culture without thereby reifying cultural difference, and the chapter explores this conundrum through an examination of particular legal judgments. This is a new chapter, written originally for a German-language collection.

2

Multiculturalism, universalism and the claims of democracy

Feminism is about change. It challenges the existing pattern of relations between the sexes, wherever these are characterized by subordination and inequality. In doing so, it necessarily takes issue with the customs and practices of existing societies. Feminists have pursued different priorities and disagreed over short-term strategies and, often enough, in their formulations of long-term goals. But whatever conclusions have been reached about the conditions for a sexually egalitarian society, most have seen these as applying beyond the confines of their own immediate world. If certain things are necessary for men and women to be equal in one society, then surely the same things must be necessary for men and women wherever they are?

This suggests that feminism is committed to a strongly universalist discourse of rights and equality – and if cultural relativism were the only alternative to universalism, this suggestion would surely be right. I take cultural relativism to be the view that norms of justice are always relative to the society in which they are formed, reflecting values and practices that vary enormously from one society to another; that there is no 'truth' outside these various local standpoints; and that it is therefore inappropriate to take the norms that emerge within one society as the measure against which to assess the practices of another. The value of this position is that it captures the situated nature of any principles of justice, the way ideals like equality or autonomy or democracy become more or less prominent depending on historical conditions, and the way the previously unthinkable becomes possible as these conditions change. To take just the more obvious examples, there was a long period of time when people found it almost impossible to conceive of slaves as sharing a common humanity with freemen, or of women as entitled to the same rights and consideration as their male counterparts; one reading of this, most notably by Marx, is that it was only as the evolution of market society made people more interchangeable that it became possible to think of them as in some sense equals. Whatever we make of this particular reading (I find it rather plausible), ideals are always formed in a context, and that context shapes and limits what people are able to conceive.

But while cultural relativism grasps at a truth about the contextual nature of principles of justice, it does so in a way that seriously overstates the incommensurability of the discourses that arise in contemporary societies, and wrongly represents the difference between cultures as a difference between hermetically sealed, internally self-consistent wholes. As Seyla Benhabib has argued, it gives the impression that a 'culture' coincides with a society, which in turn coincides with a nation (or nation of origin).[1] In doing so, it ignores the multiplicity of cultures with which any one person is associated, some of which will be very locally circumscribed, others associated with their political identifications or occupational positions, while others still (like religion) extend way beyond the boundaries of a single nation state. Cultural relativism suggests a degree of mutual insulation between 'us' and 'the others' that is very far from the realities of the contemporary world. It also encourages us into a troubling suspension of judgement when competing principles collide.

From a gender perspective, this last is a particularly pressing concern, for norms of justice are not formulated under conditions of gender equality. The 'society' that generates and authorizes existing norms is never an innocent subject; on the contrary, since no society yet operates under conditions of gender justice, what is considered to be right and just within any given society must always be open to critical scrutiny. We do not have to hypothesize a standpoint outside all society (the famous 'view from nowhere') to see how this process can occur. Sometimes the criticisms arise internally, from what are perceived to be inconsistencies between rhetoric and reality, or the failure to extend to one group of citizens rights and possibilities that have been regarded as entirely appropriate for others. In a world of rapid and extensive global communication, many of the criticisms will be provoked by comparison with principles endorsed elsewhere. We often draw on the experiences and values of other groups and societies to scrutinize prevailing understandings and formulate alternative norms.

Cultural relativism is not a useful ally for feminism, but the very reasons that make cultural relativism so unattractive have posed problems for universalism as well. If feminists have been peculiarly sensitive to the dangers in elevating existing cultural understandings to the status of unquestioned norms, they have been equally (and rightly) sensitive to the way these cultural understandings shape what are then presented as universal principles of justice and truth. Much of the work of feminist philosophers and political theorists over recent decades has been devoted to exposing the 'false' universalisms of mainstream theory: the elevation of a self-owning (masculine) individual as the supposed subject of liberal contract theory;[2] the association of universality with impartiality, and the injunction this places on subordinated social groups to put their own 'partial' needs to one side;[3] the cultivation of conceptions of rationality and justice that expel any element of emotion or care.[4] In some cases, the object of the argument has been to develop a different understanding of universalism that detaches it from its masculine provenance. In others, there has been a more trenchant critique of the very possibility of universal theory or norms. In all cases, feminists have raised problems with the way the norms and perspectives of particular social groups (largely male) come to claim the authority of 'universal' truth. I do not intend to rehearse these more philosophical arguments here. The point to stress is that those concerned with gender justice have good reason to distrust what currently pass as 'universal' principles and norms.

Since one of the problems that arises in discussion of this is that universal discourses of rights and equality often fail to engage adequately with difference, there is an obvious area of overlap between the problems encountered in achieving gender justice and those posed by justice between different cultures. One of the critiques of universalism is that it looks to a common core of humanity behind all the (supposedly contingent) differences of class, gender, ethnicity, religion or race, and that in doing so it tends to equate equality with sameness, and thereby leaves untouched systemic inequalities in power. Part of this (the least problematic part) restates an older objection associated with socialist critiques of liberalism, to the effect that an equality of rights will generate inequality when it pays no attention to background conditions. Grand assertions about all individuals having the equal right to hold on to their property turn rather sour when one individual owns only the clothes she stands up in and another owns the Microsoft empire. In similar fashion, asserting the equal right of women and men to employment can end up pretty empty when the prevailing arrangement of familial and domestic responsibilities prevents most women from exercising this right. When understood as a claim about the basic human rights to which all human beings are entitled, universalism then promises more than it can deliver. In extending to all the same set of rights and guarantees, it obscures (and may in some circumstances reinforce) those background inequalities that continue to generate inequalities of power.

This first part of the argument points to hugely contentious political questions, but is not, at a philosophical level, such a devastating critique. The political implication is that some groups may need different rights or guarantees from others in order to achieve the same kind of equalities: that there is not a single list of entitlements that should be applied in the same way to all individuals, and often a compelling case for local variation. It may be, for example, that societies need to introduce specific guarantees for the political representation of women – perhaps reserved seats for women, or a minimum quota for women candidates – in order to combat the background inequalities that would otherwise exclude women from political influence and power. Or it may be that societies need to provide additional resources and opportunities for minority ethnic groups, in order to combat a history of marginalization; and that, in so doing, they may have to modify what would otherwise be universally applicable regulations for entry to university or the civil service.

This is politically contentious, but not yet at odds with universalism per se. The proposed remedies may well involve interim modification of universal rules and practices – no simple schedule of universal rights and equalities, perhaps differential rather than identical rights – but the overall objective may still be that all groups and individuals should end up with the same conditions. The argument reminds us that universalism has to be nuanced by a better understanding of disparities in income or power, and suggests that one way of dealing with these disparities is to treat different groups differently. It does not otherwise take issue with the idea that the same rights should be universally enjoyed by all. A second, more challenging, objection is that there are some differences that will always be there, and that many of these are differences we value and want to sustain. At one level, this is so obvious it is hard to see how anyone could have overlooked it. No conceivable scenario for social change is going to eliminate in their entirety all the differences between women and men. That this obvious point was so long overlooked reflects the dominance of class in previous critical thinking, for when one focuses on class as the central measure of inequality, it becomes more plausible to think of processes of elimination or suspension that either remove the difference or make it irrelevant to the distribution of rights and power. When extended to gender, race or sexuality, this approach becomes less compelling. Women do not want their acceptance into the world of equals to be made conditional on others not noticing whether they are female or male (as if the femaleness is something to be ashamed of); and the same clearly goes for those whose skin colour or sexuality marks them out as a minority group within their society. An equality that depends on others ignoring or overlooking key features of our identity is not an acceptable option. It has to be possible to be both different and equal.

Here too, the tension with universalism may be more apparent than real (universalism is more closely associated with the idea that all individuals should have the same rights or protections or entitlements than the idea that all individuals should end up the same), but it is at this point that we edge into parallel arguments that have been developed in relation to cultural subordination. Sexual difference has almost always been associated with inequality: what marks women as different from men is also taken to mark them as of lesser value. The history of cultural difference is in some ways less depressing, already throwing up occasional examples of that more egalitarian respect for difference that has mostly evaded the relationship between the sexes. We often find ourselves intrigued, and sometimes positively impressed, by what we discover to be the different practices associated with different cultures, and there is a long history of individuals seeking to embrace cultures that are very different from their own. But cultural difference, like sexual difference, still resonates with images of superiority and inferiority. Indeed, those who seek to embrace a different culture sometimes end up in a patronizing relationship to their new-found communities, feeling that those born into the cultures do not sufficiently appreciate or understand the strengths of their own way of life.

Cultural difference is more often read as cultural hierarchy than cultural variation. There are said to be 'better' and 'worse', 'more advanced' and 'more backward' cultures. Given this history, the deployment of universal principles as a measure for judging the practices and values of other cultures begins to look rather suspect: yet another case of those 'false' universalisms that draw on the practices and values of one group for the delineation of supposedly universal rules, refuse to recognize the legitimacy of difference, and seek to impose the practices of the dominant group. Many feminists will sympathize with this suspicion, noting the parallels with their own experiences of gender. The twist in this case is that one of the key measures currently employed to differentiate 'better' and 'worse', 'more advanced' and 'more backward' cultures is their treatment of women: whether they practise forms of genital mutilation that deny women (but not men) the enjoyment of their sexuality; whether they allow men (but never women) to have multiple marriage partners; whether they insist on the confinement of women to the home or the veiling of women when they go out in public; whether they insist on the segregation of the sexes in education or religious worship.

This is the issue that has surfaced in recent debates on the tensions between feminism and multiculturalism. Some feminists (myself included) perceive a close family relationship between feminism and multiculturalism: see these as linked, not just because both tackle issues of inequality and oppression, but more deeply, because the oppressions they address share a common structure. In each case, the failure to recognize people as equals seems to be bound up in some way with the inability to accept difference. It is assumed that those marked by difference (and it is always the people on the margins who get marked by their difference while the others are somehow seen as the norm) should bring themselves into line with the others in their society in order to be included as full members.

This generates a strong coincidence of concerns between those pursuing sexual and those pursuing cultural equality, linked to a shared critique of the universalisms that have falsely generalized from one sex or one culture, and a shared perception that equality may depend on greater respect for / recognition of difference. For many feminists, the coincidence of concerns is reinforced by the knowledge that Western feminism too often read the world off the experience of white middle-class women, a knowledge learnt through a lengthy period of internal critique and re-assessment which revolved around the very different experiences and priorities of women depending on their class, race, ethnicity, religion or nationality. These shared concerns fostered what might otherwise seem an unlikely alliance of feminism and multiculturalism. But when this alliance makes it impossible for women identified with one culture to criticize what they regard as the sexually oppressive practices of another, this can lead to a form of cultural relativism that is not, I have suggested, compatible with feminist politics. So how to deal with this issue? Can feminists working in international organizations confidently draw up a schedule of basic women's rights that they then present as a requirement for all societies? Can feminists from a majority culture in a multicultural society take it on themselves to criticize what they see as the sexually inegalitarian practices of minority cultural groups? Can feminists from a minority culture take it on themselves to challenge the practices of a majority group?

Despite my earlier reservation about treating cultural difference as a matter of 'us' and 'the others', I have posed this as a question about the critics from 'outside'. This is because it seems to me too easy to resolve the tension by pointing to the many women inside each 'culture' contesting its understandings of women's position. In those parts of Africa where genital cutting is most widely practised, there are many women's groups that have campaigned long and hard to get the practice declared illegal, and then campaign equally long and hard to get their governments to enforce the legislation. There are women activists across India working to publicize instances of dowry murder, campaigning for the employment rights of secluded women, and battling against the heavy weight of cultural practices that tie women's existence to oppressive notions of family honour and legitimate continuing sexual violence. In Britain, groups like Southall Black Sisters work inside as well as outside Muslim communities to challenge the power differential between men and women; and there are women within all the churches and religions organizing for greater equity between the sexes in the practices of their religion. This history of internal contestation reinforces what should be the starting point for thinking about issues of multiculturalism: that cultures are not monolithic, are always in the process of interpretation and re-interpretation, and never immune to change. But I do not think we should rely on these observations to close off discussion of the 'hard case' scenario of external critique – as if criticism is legitimate when we can identify internal critics but not otherwise allowed.

Tensions between sexual and cultural equality

In the most influential recent statement of the conditions for multicultural citizenship, Will Kymlicka argues that the case for minority cultural rights is entirely consistent with universalism so long as it is conceived on a relatively weak model.[5] His first point is that the claims of minority cultures are justified precisely through reference to the universal rights of individuals, for if all individuals are to have the same rights and capacities for choosing how to lead their lives, and culture provides (as he argues) the context within which individuals can make meaningful choices, then members of minority cultures need the security of their own cultures in order to enjoy the same individual rights as others. The second point is that we should distinguish between the stronger self-government rights of indigenous peoples who have been involuntarily incorporated into a larger unit by conquest or colonization, and the lesser 'polyethnic' rights of immigrant groups that have voluntarily uprooted themselves; the case for the former does not spill over into a case for the latter.[6] His third point is that we should distinguish between the 'external protections' that may prove necessary to secure the rights of minority cultures vis-à-vis other cultural groups, and the 'internal restrictions' that illegitimately constrain individual members. Multicultural accommodation, in this view, does not mean that groups are to be allowed to discriminate amongst their members on the grounds of sex, race or sexual preference.

At first glance, this would seem to resolve any tensions between sexual and cultural equality. In their pursuit of equal citizenship, societies need to recognize more fully the rights of minority cultures, but any resulting policies of accommodation should be curtailed by reference to standard liberal guarantees on the rights of individuals. Whatever powers are delegated to the group in question, these must not be such that they violate the rights of its women members. So far, so good, but on closer examination Kymlicka's solution looks less satisfactory. First, it is not always so easy to distinguish between the legitimate 'external protections' and the illegitimate 'internal restrictions'. As Ayelet Shachar has argued, one of the main concerns of identity groups vis-à-vis other groups or the state is to retain the authority to decide who is a group member: to decide, for example, who counts as a Jew, or who is to be recognized as a member of a particular indigenous group.[7] This authority operates primarily through family law, which can then involve significant restrictions on the rights of women members. In many cases, the criteria for membership have been self-evidently discriminatory, as when Indian tribes in North American reservations have recognized the children of men who marry outside the group as full members, but not the children of women who marry outside. It is not always possible to draw a line between the external rights of the group and the internal rights of its members. Depending on how generously we interpret the first, they may well conflict with the second.

The further problem arises when Kymlicka considers the conditions in which the state could reasonably act against discrimination within a cultural group. 'Obviously', he notes, 'intervention is justified in the case of gross and systematic violation of human rights, such as slavery or genocide or mass torture and expulsions',[8] and in the case of newly arriving immigrant groups, he does not think it wrong 'for liberal states to insist that immigration entails accepting the legitimacy of state enforcement of liberal principles, so long as immigrants know this in advance and none the less voluntarily choose to come'.[9] This still leaves a very large area open to debate. At this point, Kymlicka backs away from what might be conceived as a coercive imposition of liberal principles on minority groups, arguing that, if there is a consensus within the community on the legitimacy of restricting individual rights, it may not be appropriate for governments to intervene. The theoretical protections for women then dissolve in the face of worries about imposition, and it seems that only 'gross and systematic violation' will qualify for action. We know, however, that much of the discrimination against women will fail this test, being of its nature more informal, 'private' and covert. Much of it, moreover, will have become 'naturalized' over the years, to the extent where even those most discriminated against may accept their conditions as legitimate and just. As Condorcet remarked in his *Essay on the Political Rights of Women*: 'Custom may familiarize mankind with the violation of their natural rights to such an extent, that even among those who have lost or been deprived of these rights, no one thinks of reclaiming them, or is even conscious that they have suffered any injustice.'

It is in this context that Susan Moller Okin poses the question: 'Is multiculturalism bad for women?'[10] The questions she raises are primarily addressed to the internal politics of societies made up of a number of cultural groups (questions of cultural respect within countries, rather than between them); and the aspect of multiculturalism that most concerns her is the claim that minority cultures or ways of life are not sufficiently protected by guaranteeing the individual rights of their members, but should also be protected through special group rights or privileges. Examples include the decision of the French government in the 1980s to extend the normal understanding of marital dependant so as to enable immigrant men (from certain cultures) to bring multiple wives into the country; and the exemption of minority groups in Britain from a variety of legal regulations that might otherwise be construed as imposing a discriminatory burden on them. (The most quoted of these is the exemption of turban-wearing Sikhs from safety regulations that require motorbike riders to wear a helmet.) Further examples would include the recognition of customary (religious) law in countries like India, where worries about the political effects of imposing standardized legislation on Muslim and Hindu alike produced a range of religion-specific Acts to regulate marriage, divorce and succession arrangements for the different religious communities; or the delegation of marriage and divorce affairs in Israel to the autonomous courts of the different religious communities.

In these cases, sensitivity to ethnic or religious difference has meant a modification of what would otherwise be universally applicable regulations and rules. Often enough, these exemptions allow for greater inequality between women and men. Okin argues that 'we – especially those of us who consider ourselves politically progressive and opposed to all forms of oppression – have been too quick to assume that feminism and multiculturalism are both good things which are easily reconciled'.[11] In her analysis, there are more often tensions than compatibilities, and we then have to decide whether to prioritize cultural group rights or women's equality. Though this might seem an uncontroversial position within feminism, reactions to Okin have been mixed – perhaps most notably among feminists. I note here three recurrent objections.

Appealing to principles that are also negated by Western societies

One objection is that the criticism of minority cultural practice appeals to principles of equality and autonomy that are also being negated by practices in the majority culture, that Western societies have a poor record on women's rights and equalities, and that one should put one's own house in order before trying to sort out anyone else's. The critique of polygamy or arranged marriages or the enforced seclusion of women gives the impression that all is well in the heart-lands of liberal democracy. Since women in the most developed societies continue to suffer from inequalities of pay and employment, from gross violations of their bodily integrity through rape and domestic violence, and a persistent devaluation of their sex as reflected in cultural and political representation, the implied contrast with majority cultural practice is deeply disingenuous.

I think there are circumstances in which this would be a valid complaint. I have often been struck by the dishonesty of those who draw on the language of sexual equality to characterize Muslim communities in Europe and elsewhere as alien, backward, premodern – but otherwise exhibit no interest in sexual equality. In such circumstances, one cannot but think that the real agenda is racism rather than a high-minded concern for the rights of Muslim women. The complaint is hardly valid, however, as applied to feminists who have spent most of their lives campaigning against what they see as gender injustices in their own society. Nor, to push this further, is it so obvious that people must 'earn' the right to speak out against injustice by first demonstrating their track record closer to home. If they have not done so, we may query their complacency; we may doubt their grasp of gender issues; and may sometimes want to question their real agenda. But even in the worst instances, where highlighting injustice elsewhere is primarily about claiming the superiority of one's own society or group, there may still be an injustice to address.

Appealing to principles that are themselves open to critique

This second objection returns us to the worries about universalism, and whether the principles employed to criticize the cultural practices of others are just a glorified version of the principles that underpin one's own. Prioritizing the rights of individuals over the rights of groups, for example, may reflect a particular conception of the relationship between the individual and his/her community that values personal autonomy and mobility over the ties of family or community, sees freedom as 'freedom from' the constraints of tradition, and attaches little weight to the sense of belonging to a particular community or group. This conception of human freedom has been linked historically to the evolution of market society, which values individuals by their contribution to production rather than their status in the social order, and often requires them to detach themselves from family, community or country in their pursuit of work. The detached and autonomous individual then becomes the focus for liberal ideals of freedom and equality, but it may be that the high value liberals attach to autonomy illegitimately takes what has become a central preoccupation of Western cultures and turns it into a universal norm.[12]

This problem surfaces even in the most promising versions of liberal thought. In making her case for the capabilities approach, for example, Martha Nussbaum argues that the language of capabilities is less strongly linked to a particular cultural and historical tradition than the language of rights, and not therefore so vulnerable to complaints about cultural specificity.[13] Yet the more content she has put into the notion of capabilities, the less plausible this claim appears, while the centrality she attaches to ensuring the conditions for individual choice still leaves it open to the standard objection. Whether we operate with a language of capabilities or a language of rights, questions of historical provenance will continue to arise. I would argue, however, that we should see these questions as cautioning us against the dogmatic presumption to exclusive truth, not as ruling certain principles out of court because of the context in which they arose. That principles of rights or justice emerge and change through time is, I think, beyond question. That they often express and legitimate the partial experiences of particular societies – and, as many feminists would add, of particular groups within particular societies – also seems to me beyond question; and one consequence of this is that all principles of justice have to be regarded as open to contestation, revision and critique. But questions of historical provenance do not settle which norms are the most defensible, and there are certain elements in the liberal conception of freedom and equality – including its insistence on the separateness of each individual and the dangers of subsuming the needs of women under the 'greater good' of the family or community or state – that feminists would be ill advised to abandon.[14]

My own view is that the liberal tradition is still deeply flawed by the priority it gives to choice over equality, by its uncritical endorsement of what can be a coercive notion of autonomy, and its all too frequent conception of the individual as 'owner' of his/her self. But the debate on this continues within what are regarded as liberal cultures as well as those regarded as non-liberal. If it would be mistaken on the one side to dismiss liberalism as just the local prejudice of the West, it would be equally mistaken to treat it as a foreign import that has no purchase in Africa or Asia or the Middle East. The issue we should be focusing on is the tension between sexual and cultural equality: whether the requirements of gender justice (however we come to define these) come into conflict with the requirements of justice between cultural groups, and, if so, whether we have to resolve this by giving priority to one over the other. Displacing this onto a debate about liberalism – one side defending its superior conception of justice, the other pointing out its incipient tendencies towards cultural imperialism – is not the best way to promote such a discussion. On the contrary, it may unwittingly reinforce what Richard Bellamy describes as 'a widespread liberal prejudice that pluralist objections to liberalism derive solely from illiberal throwbacks miraculously marooned in the modern world'.[15] While doubts about liberalism are often justified, it is not useful to turn a debate about gender and cultural justice into a debate that places feminism/liberalism on the one side and multiculturalism on the other. In this context, the source of the ideals is less pressing than whether they provide adequate guides to policy.

Failing to understand the social meaning of different practices

A third objection levelled at Okin is that her understanding of the practices she criticizes is constrained by her 'outsider' status, and that, particularly in her critique of the religious practices that segregate women from men and enforce their subordination, she overstates the patriarchalism of what she describes. I am not primarily concerned with whether this is a fair criticism of Okin, but more with the underlying issue of who is in the best position to understand.

There are three sub-issues here. The first relates to the observation in the last section about misreading objections to liberalism as 'illiberal throwbacks miraculously marooned in the modern world'. Against this perception, I find it more compelling to read contemporary assertions of cultural, religious or ethnic identity, and their associated demands for recognition, as a quintessentially modern phenomenon. One only has to think of the recent movements against secularism in India, the Islamist revival of the last decades, or the 're-discovery' of ethnic and religious identities in the former Yugoslavia to recognize that cultural and religious identities are coming to matter in a new way. Within Europe, one might also look at the tensions that arise between first- and second-generation immigrants, and the bewilderment of parents who worked hard to assimilate with the dominant culture when their children now reject this. Global migration is intensifying problems of group inequality within countries, often along the faultline of ethnic or religious difference, while between countries, globalization and its associated 'sharp shocks' have generated counter-movements that frequently mobilize along cultural and religious lines. Within this, women are often significant players.

The second point is that we do not understand social practices unless we understand the social meanings with which they are invested, and that critics from outside a particular cultural setting are often too ready to dismiss what they do not understand. I have never heard a plausible version of this that makes me less critical of genital cutting, and have found it hard to sympathize with explanations of polygamy when these invariably explain why men should have mul-

tiple wives rather than women having multiple husbands. But I certainly see that a critique of arranged marriage fails to differentiate
between marriages forced on unwilling partners and marriages
arranged by parents concerned with their children's best interests;
and that veiling can contest the sexual commodification of women
even while confirming unveiled women as sexually loose. A number
of respondents to Okin's essay have stressed what they see as her lack
of sympathy for religion, and that gulf between believers and non-
believers – even greater, it often seems, than the gulf between those
who follow different religions – is indeed one of the more difficult
ones for the social critic to bridge. There are limits to what we can
ask of the social critic: we clearly cannot insist that people engage in
a particular practice or embrace a particular set of beliefs before
venturing any judgement. But differences in culture and religion have
provided a particularly fertile ground for misunderstanding, and it is
likely that many of the initial judgements will prove too simple or
too harsh.

Against both these points is a third issue that concerns the tendency of all human beings to make the best of a bad job (Condorcet's
point). It must surely be that 'insiders' can claim a deeper understanding of their social meanings and social practices, but they may also
be so thoroughly subordinated by their conditions that they are
unable to recognize any injustice. Though this edges disturbingly
close to notions of 'false consciousness', I would defend it as an
indispensable component in feminist thought. Sexual oppression is
not justified by the generations of women who have put up with it;
nor is it justified by them saying that the silencing of women in public
or the unequal division of domestic labour is 'natural' and right. We
know that people living in unjust or impoverished conditions adjust
their expectations downwards in order to survive and remain sane;
we know that women can live their lives by images of femininity that
do immense damage to their self-esteem; we know that people living
in relations of domination often find it hard to imagine themselves
living under anything else. Perceptions of what is desirable are always
shaped and constrained by perceptions of what is possible, and the
fact that a woman living in a society where women have always taken
the responsibility for children and household may think it unnatural
for men to take an equal share does not require us to suspend our
critique of the sexual division of labour. Similarly, the fact that
women living in societies where girls are considered unmarriageable
if they freely enjoy their sexuality may insist on the genital mutilation
of their daughters does not require us to regard the practice as what

they freely 'choose'. Choices are made within particular social constraints, and much of the time we are not even aware that other
choices were possible. If so, this suggests that those most subordinated may also be those least able to recognize the injustice of their
position. It may then be the outsiders, not insiders, who are best
placed to judge.

This is not a comfortable conclusion, and clearly has to be moderated by the earlier points about the tendency to misrepresent current
tensions as episodes in the battle between modernity and tradition,
and the likely misreading of social practices and values by those who
can only view them from outside. In most cases, the starkness of the
conclusion is further moderated by the presence of internal critics
who do not accept their conditions as either natural or just, but I
have argued that this last cannot be the decisive consideration. Criticism will certainly be better informed when there are internal as well
as external critics, and the resulting dialogue may well lead to a different understanding of values and rights. We should not, however,
conclude that there is nothing to be said about abuses of women's
rights until these abuses have been challenged from inside. We should
not, as Martha Nussbaum observes, allow the fears of a 'do-gooder
colonialism' to block initiatives towards gender justice.[16]

Equalizing women's power

All the above is by way of preamble and clarification: setting out the
reasons for anticipating both alliance and tension between feminism
and multiculturalism; arguing the dangers of cultural relativism but
also the legitimate concerns about universalism; challenging the
paralysis that sometimes sets in when confronted with cultural claims.
Let me restate some key points:

(1) Cultural relativism, understood as the belief that norms of
     justice are relative to the society in which they are formed, and
     that it is inappropriate to take the norms that emerge within
     one society as the measure against which to assess the practices
     of others, is not a useful way forward. At the same time:
(2) Principles of justice are always formed in a particular historical
     context, and often reflect the preoccupations of more powerful
     groups. This does not prevent such principles from having a
     universal application, but it does mean they must always be
     regarded as open to contestation, reformulation and change.

(3) Cultural reification, understood as the belief that 'cultures' are monolithic, internally self-consistent and externally sealed off from other influences, is not a plausible way of understanding the world.

(4) The social meaning and significance of cultural practices are best understood by those who engage in them, and it is all too easy for 'outsiders' to misread them. At the same time:

(5) The social construction of preferences and aspirations suggests that those most oppressed by a particular practice may also be the least well equipped to recognize its inegalitarian character. Evidence of internal support or consensus is not decisive, and a 'hands-off' approach to cultural difference can end up capitulating to unjust social power.

Since principles of justice are always potentially skewed by the conditions of their formulation, and the understanding of social practices is always open to re-interpretation in the light of new knowledges and experience, one important implication is that both principles and policies should be worked out with the fullest possible involvement of all relevant groups. So not just the 'global citizens' working to define human rights or principles of justice, nor yet the religious and cultural leaders representing the principles of 'their' culture or religion, but also the more hidden constituencies with what may be their very different experiences and perspectives and concerns. In seeking to establish which rights should be regarded as inalienable or which practices are inimical to equality between women and men, it is not possible to rely on simple deduction from supposedly universal principles. We always need the maximum possible dialogue to counter the false universalisms that have so dogged previous practice, as well as the 'substitutionism' that has allowed certain groups to present themselves as spokespeople for the rest. The persistent under-representation of women in most of the forums in which these issues are addressed then emerges as a particularly pressing problem. This leads us to what I have elsewhere described as a 'politics of presence' to ensure full participation of all those concerned.[17]

I do not mean by this that matters of basic principle are to be settled by majority vote, and I shall return shortly to reasons why democratization alone is not enough of an answer. But it is only in relatively rare circumstances that policy disagreements involve fundamental issues of principle – pitting equality, for example, against inequality, or the right to life against the right to kill. More commonly, disagreements revolve around competing interpretations of such principles, as in the famous disputes about when a foetus becomes a human being, and whether it has an independent right to life. Even if we start (as I would recommend) from an unashamed commitment to equality, this often turns out to settle surprisingly little. It can be argued, for example, that equality means desegregation: no separate spheres for men and women, no separate enclaves for white and black. But there is often a compelling egalitarian case for segregation, as when people suggest that, in the context of current gender relations, girls will get more equal attention from their teachers and a more equal opportunity to advance their education if they are taught in single-sex schools; or that in a context of racist attacks, ethnic minority groups will enjoy more equal security when they are able to concentrate in the same neighbourhood rather than being dispersed throughout a wider community. The French 'affaire des foulards' (when Muslim girls were banned from wearing headscarves in school) was argued in competing discourses of equality: on the one hand, that all citizens should be equally bound by the same principles of secularism; on the other, that it was unfair to prevent Muslim students from wearing a symbol of their religion when Catholic schoolgirls were permitted to wear the crucifixes that symbolized their own.

The requirements of equality are rarely transparent, and sorting them out is not just a matter of the depth of one's commitment or the clarity of one's thought. It also matters where one is coming from, what kind of experience one brings to bear on the issue, and from what kind of position one speaks. Perspectives matter, for, consciously or not, all of us draw on local knowledge and past experience in making our political judgements, and we often reach contrasting conclusions depending on our location in hierarchies of power. When national governments contest what they see as the intrusiveness of international agencies, they often make the point that schedules of rights have been drawn up by the more powerful nations and do not adequately reflect their own rather different experiences. They rarely, however, go on to recognize the further implication about the way their own understandings have been formed: the dominance of particular groups in defining what counts as 'traditional' culture, and the persistent under-representation of women's voices in identifying what is defensible and fair. Social customs that reflect patterns of male dominance are often wrongly represented as part of what 'the society' wants to sustain. Where this happens, cultural claims can become a vehicle for maintaining the subordination of women.

The case for equalizing women's access to decision-making arenas is therefore closely bound up with the issues explored in this volume. Women need equality of political and policy representation for a whole range of reasons: as a straightforward matter of fairness between the sexes; so as to provide more vigorous advocacy for interests that would otherwise be overlooked; so as to challenge the infantilization that regards women as better looked after by the (supposedly) more knowledgeable men. All these are substantial reasons in themselves. The crucial addition is that societies cannot confidently establish which policies are most just without the equal involvement of women and men, young and old – of the less as well as the more powerful members of the society. Basic principles are often very basic, not really saying much about how they are to be interpreted and applied. The safe translation from principle to policy is heavily dependent on local knowledge and differences of perspective, and policy prescriptions that are arrived at without the full involvement of all social groups are always open to doubt. When women are excluded from (or just significantly under-represented in) decision-making assemblies and forums, we cannot but suspect the supposed universalism of the policies that then emerge, and this applies a fortiori to the self-defined voices of any 'community' or 'culture'. Equalizing the power of men and women in the processes of policy-formation and decision-making has to be seen as central to resolving the tensions discussed here – central, but not, of itself, the solution. There is an understandable tendency among those tussling with issues of multiculturalism and universalism to look to the democratization of debate as the solution, to insist that principles must be formulated in dialogue, that women's participation will be crucial in challenging monolithic representations of cultural traditions, and that competing voices must be heard. My argument so far falls broadly within this pattern, but I do not want to suggest that democratization is enough of an answer, or that we should drop the philosophical meanderings about universality and concentrate on getting more women involved.

There is always an element of utopianism in appealing to democratic participation to solve all our problems, for who in her wildest dreams expects the right kind of egalitarian democracy to occur? If we set the conditions at too high a level – only recognizing as legitimate, for example, what emerges from the full and equal participation of men and women, young and old, more and less powerful across the globe – we will end up in precisely the kind of paralysis I want to argue against. We would probably be unable to recognize the legitimacy of *any* cultural rights, for there would always be issues about whether the voices of the community or culture in question were genuinely representative. Nor would we be able to settle *any* policies for sexual equality, for there would always be a question mark over the inclusiveness of the decision-making process through which the policies emerged. This is not where I want to end up. We have to aim at a 'good-enough' democracy, rather than paralysing ourselves with an impossible ideal, and my argument should be seen as a case for more extensive consultation – and more equal representation – rather than a statement about the only conditions under which gender justice could emerge.

A further complication derives from the 'on the one hand / on the other hand' pairing that notes the insights 'insiders' will bring to the social meaning and significance of their cultural practices, but sets this against the social construction of preferences and aspirations that can make it hard for those most oppressed by a particular practice to recognize it as unfair. I think it highly unlikely that a discussion conducted on genuinely inclusive lines would fail to throw up evidence of internal opposition to practices that constrained women's freedom or subjected them to arbitrary male power; and I think this particularly unlikely in the light of what I have argued about the inter-penetration of different cultures and different ethical ideals. I also believe that the very process of inclusion encourages people to stretch their sense of what is desirable and possible, enabling them to articulate previously repressed interests and concerns. But what if all this is too starry-eyed? What if there still turns out to be no internal contestation, or the dissident voices that are raised turn out to be regarded as unrepresentative by the vast majority of women? Should 'outsiders' then reassure themselves with the notion that practices are legitimate because hardly anyone engaged in them states an objection? Should they restrict themselves to condemning only policies that are being actively contested from inside?

Modesty is not always a virtue, and important as it is to challenge the arrogance of those who believe they can settle everything from first principles, this line of inaction would be taking modesty too far. I do not, that is, think we can close off discussion of what I have termed the 'hard case' scenario of external critique. Democratization should be regarded as a crucial element in tackling tensions between multiculturalism and women's equality, but democratization sometimes becomes indefinite postponement, and is better regarded as part, rather than all, of the solution. Despite the questions I have raised about the shaky basis on which supposedly universal principles get formed, there is no getting away from guiding principles as a way of identifying which practices are most indefensible and most at odds with sexual equality concerns.

The ones I offer here are not particularly original: harm is one; equality a second; and whether people enjoy substantive conditions for choice is a third. Though the harm that is done to people by the various practices enjoined on them is always contestable – what I regard as harmful will not always coincide with what you think most damaging to a person's well-being or self-esteem – this contestability should not blind us to questions of degree. Harm varies in grievous- ness and reversibility: this is presumably what Will Kymlicka has in mind when he identifies the 'gross and systematic violations' of slavery, genocide or mass torture as legitimating external interven- tion, and intimates a range of lesser violations that liberal societies might have to condone. My own list would be somewhat longer and would certainly include the irreversible violation of bodily integrity involved in rape or genital cutting, or the sometimes reversible but still gross harm of being forced into a marriage against one's will. There are certain harms that are sufficiently grievous to override worries about the legitimacy of any one person's understanding, and do not allow for indefinite postponement until full consultation has occurred. In the messy world of real politics, it is important to retain a sense of scale, for even if all harms are philosophically contestable, some are patently more compelling than others. Here, too, we should aim at 'good-enough' discriminations, and not set the standards of rigour so high as to paralyse any kind of action.

Harm addresses the content of a practice; the equality principle asks whether it is permitted for both women and men. One might set aside, for example, the question of whether it is better for people to have one or many (or no) marriage partners, or whether this is some- thing that can be usefully discussed by any except the individuals involved. If the laws of a society permit men to have multiple mar- riage partners but do not extend the same latitude to women, there is still a prima facie case for complaint: something is being presented as acceptable for one sex but entirely illegitimate for the other. In this context, the formality often associated with the equality principle (and criticized as such by many feminists) works to its advantage, for it is not necessary to take up a position on the content of the practice, only whether it applies equally to both women and men.

The third principle addresses an issue that has recurred throughout my argument, which is whether we can take consent as evidence that there is no problem, or should also be considering the substantive conditions that enable people to choose. Political theorists sometimes refer to the distinction between 'voice' and 'exit' as different ways of getting at people's preferences and choice: so sometimes we explicitly voice our approval or dissatisfaction, perhaps through voting or writing or participating in a political campaign; other times we show what we think by getting up and going away. Either can be taken as evidence that certain practices are consensual, for, if no one has either objected or left, there can't be very much of a problem. As applied to the situation of many women around the world (and I include here some of the most developed liberal democracies), this offers far too rosy a vision, for neither voice nor exit is an easy option if you live in daily fear of physical abuse and see no prospect of earning a living outside your present community. So while it is hardly appropriate for one person or group to dictate to another what they 'ought' to be choosing, it can also be inappropriate to take silence as evidence of consent. Choice depends on substantive conditions. These include, at a minimum, having the political and civil freedoms that enable one to 'voice' an objection, and the educational and employment opportunities that make 'exit' a genuine choice.

With each of these principles, the devil is in the detail, and there is an (entirely defensible) circularity that returns us to the democratic agenda. As the harm continuum stretches out, for example, beyond the more extreme cases of grievous bodily harm, there will be numerous instances where the issues are far from obvious – either because there is genuine uncertainty over the harm involved, or because its scale seems too indecisive to justify sacrificing other values. I have already mentioned the case of segregated education, which is arguably something that harms girls and boys by restricting their communication with members of the opposite sex and encouraging an ideology of separate spheres, but is also arguably of benefit to both in promoting more favourable conditions for learning. Or consider the harm that is done to women whose religion denies them the opportunity to serve as priests or rabbis. I might feel that this is unquestionably a harm, or might suspend judgement on the content of the harm and simply note the inequality that permits to men an opportunity that it simultaneously denies to women. But I might still want to weigh these considerations against the harm done to religions if they are forced by legislative intervention to standardize their arrangements for worship and comply with equal opportunities law.[18]

The uncertainties thrown up in the application of general principles to specific cases bring us back to the necessity for inclusive participation, for these uncertainties are best resolved when all relevant groups are fully engaged in the decision-making process. Cultural claims matter: they are themselves important claims about equality, and not to be arrogantly dismissed by reference to a pre-ordained list of universal rights. But cultural claims are too often framed by a monolithic understanding of 'culture' that overstates the internal consensus and misrepresents social customs that sustain male dominance as practices 'the society' wants to sustain. The best protection against this lies in the mobilization of alternative voices, which will often throw up more nuanced readings of the tension between cultural and sexual equality, and may well modify the understanding of both. The full representation of women in discussion and decision-making is a crucial condition for settling the troubled relationship that is developing between multiculturalism and the defence of women's rights. It is important, however, not to be too starry-eyed about democracy, and not to postpone action until that ideal democracy occurs.

3

Dilemmas of gender and culture: the judge, the democrat and the political activist

The phrase 'minorities within minorities' alerts us to both parallels and potential collision. It suggests a symmetry between groups that have been minoritized by virtue of their race, ethnicity, religion, language or culture, and sub-groups within these, minoritized by virtue of age, sexuality, gender or class. If the disadvantages suffered by the larger minority give rise to legitimate claims, consistency requires us to address further disadvantages that may affect minorities within it: we cannot, in fairness, say that public authorities should tackle the injustices that attach to one group but feel under no obligation to deal with those that attach to the others. The further implication is that these two concerns may collide. In particular, actions designed to strengthen the position of a cultural or religious minority within the larger society may simultaneously strengthen the power of cultural and religious leaders over dissidents within their group. Women and young people will often bear the brunt of this. This tension has been the burden of much discussion of the relationship between feminism and multiculturalism. Multiculturalism takes issue with the monoculturalism that informs much contemporary thought and practice, stresses the diversity of the many cultures that make up contemporary societies, and argues that societies and/or governments should recognize the legitimacy of at least some cultural claims. These have ranged through appeals to the wider society to recognize the validity of a variety of norms and traditions, to calls for legislative exemptions to accommodate what would otherwise be deemed illegal practices, to the devolution of authority to cultural communities in the regulation of marital and familial affairs. Since much of what we understand by culture revolves around the expectations attached to being male and female, the understandings and practices of sexuality, and the conditions under which people marry, have children and divorce, it is evident that some of these claims could have unhappy consequences for women.

Consider polygamous marriages, which are perfectly legal in many parts of the world, but have been prohibited under English law; or marriages involving spouses under the age of sixteen, also legal in a number of jurisdictions (including some states in the USA) but prohibited by English law. One result of this is that immigration officials will refuse entry clearance to second wives or under-age spouses even when one party to the marriage is a UK citizen and the marriage is fully recognized elsewhere. The marital conventions of one culture are thereby imposed on all, and, in at least some versions of multiculturalism, this is seen as unfairly disadvantaging members of the cultural minority. Yet addressing this seeming inequity would remove what many women experience as an important protection, legitimating multiple wives for men, and making it easier for parents to pressure young girls into marriage. As Ayelet Shachar puts it, 'well-meaning accommodations aimed at mitigating power inequalities between groups may end up reinforcing power hierarchies within them'; where this happens, 'at-risk group members are being asked to shoulder a disproportionate share of the risks of multiculturalism'.[1]

And this problem is likely to intensify, for when cultural groups feel themselves under threat, perhaps precisely because of pressures to assimilate, the first sign of danger may well be an unwelcome assertiveness on the part of women or younger members. One frequent response is to re-codify the norms regulating family life in an ever more restrictive way: what Shachar has termed a 'reactive culturalism' in the face of rapid social change. Traditions are rediscovered or even created, and practices that have long been contested are restored to a central defining role. The codes regulating gender relations then become bound up with notions of cultural authenticity, and the defence of one's culture becomes in large part the defence of that culture's notions about what it is appropriate for women to do. In this context, otherwise well-intentioned moves towards recognizing the legitimacy of a multiplicity of cultures could encourage public authorities to turn a blind eye to coercive practices that institutionalize women's subordination, strengthen the power of self-styled community leaders – almost always male – who represent a very partial view of 'their' community's most cherished traditions, and lead to a paralysed relativism that puts sensitivity to cultural difference over the rights or needs of women.

The strategies adopted by political theorists for dealing with this dilemma mostly fall into one of two camps. The first is broadly judicial. It brings to bear a number of principles relating to the rights of the individual and group, and arranges these in the appropriate hierarchy in order to generate a solution. Among frequently invoked principles are the right of nations to self-determination (most commonly employed in relation to indigenous minorities), the freedom of religion, and the right of women to be treated equally with men. In much – though by no means all – of the feminist literature, this last takes priority, and sex equality then becomes a non-negotiable condition for any practices of multiculturalism. Outside this literature, sex equality tends to drop down the list. As Susan Moller Okin has noted, liberal theorists commonly rate principles of racial equality above those of religious freedom or cultural autonomy, but rarely attach comparable weight to the requirements of gender equality.[2] Meanwhile, for some critics, the very idea that a cultural group might have rights is felt to be highly contentious; and the 'minorities with minorities' dilemma is settled by rejecting the very notion of cultural minority rights.[3]

The less judicially inclined have looked to democratic deliberation as the better way of addressing value conflict, arguing that intercultural dialogue can generate a more culturally sensitive agreement on core principles of justice, or that greater democracy within each community can re-define values in ways that meet women's equality concerns.[4] This approach takes as its starting point the view that principles of justice are formed in particular historical contexts, and cannot therefore be appealed to as the *deus ex machina* to settle inter-cultural disputes. It also stresses that the most deeply held of values still remains open to change, and that seemingly incompatible value systems can come closer to resolution in the course of discussion and debate. Instead, then, of a judgment handed down via externally generated principles of justice, this approach envisages a dialogic exchange between individuals from different cultural groups. People may embark on this process with an acute sense of what differentiates them, but hopefully will discover significant common ground between their different value systems, and/or come to accept that some aspects of their own value system are harder than they thought to defend. Some versions of this have invoked a plurality of cultural communities represented by relatively uncontested cultural authorities: this seems to be the approach of Bhikhu Parekh, who calls on societies to establish mechanisms for the inter-cultural valuation of disputed practices such as polygamy or female genital mutilation, but tends to envisage the dialogue as carried out by 'minority spokesmen'.[5] Most of the feminist literature, by contrast, stresses the pluralism within as well as between communities, and argues for mechanisms of empowerment that will enable women within each group to challenge patriarchal definitions of their supposedly shared culture. In both cases, however, the emphasis is on resolution through dialogue rather than adjudication from on high.

The judicial approach has been seen as problematic because it appeals to principles of justice that may themselves be sedimented norms of a dominant culture. The deliberative approach corrects this, but, despite its more encouraging view of value resolution, can still be said to exaggerate the scale of value conflict. One of my central points in this chapter is that political theorists have promoted an over-charged understanding of the 'minorities within minorities' dilemma, simultaneously over-estimating the value conflicts associated with cultural pluralism and under-estimating the political ones. The inflation arises partly because the literature on multiculturalism has developed in close association with a literature on minority rights, which in turn has drawn heavily on the experience of indigenous peoples. As a result of this, it has inclined to the view that there are fundamentally different belief systems and fundamentally opposed principles of justice. The inflation also reflects an occupational hazard for political theorists, who like the experience of grappling with 'hard cases', and sometimes make them harder than they are in order to highlight the resolution. In many cases, however, there is no deep disagreement: no fundamentally opposed understandings of justice that have to be either ordered or democratically resolved.

What we face, rather, are complex matters of political judgement and strategy that derive their complexity from the specificities of historical context, and the often agonizing gap between the messages we intend to send out and the ones those around us receive. When people make their claims – for sex equality or minority rights or cultural recognition – they intervene on a stage already set by previous interventions, and employ discourses already mobilized to serve what may be very different ends. The history of these discourses forms the inevitable backdrop to political action, and since we cannot just assert, with Humpty Dumpty, that we will make the words mean what *we* choose, this history frames and informs our political choices. Culture, for example, can be deployed in highly opportunistic ways, as in 'cultural defences' that represent (usually non-Western) cultures as more accommodating towards rape and murder; and abuses of this kind stoke up much of the opposition to multiculturalism. The

rights of women can also become the rallying cry for projects that
have little to do with feminism, as when a discourse of sex equality
is employed to justify military intervention in Islamic countries or to
represent the backwardness of colonized peoples.[6] The discourse then
seems to assume a life of its own, often far detached from its original
uses.

We can, of course, say that the meanings others attach to our
principles are beside the point, that the task is to determine what is
right and just, and that it is no concern of ours if the arguments we
derive fuel developments in unwanted directions. But most of those
involved in political campaigns remain acutely aware that they are
making both normative and strategic judgements, assessing not only
what is 'right' but what best advances their claims in a given historical context. Many of the dilemmas associated with the 'minorities
within minorities' conundrum – and, more specifically, with the femi-
nism/multiculturalism debates – are best understood in this light, as
dilemmas that are political and contextual. They certainly involve
normative judgements, but, even when solutions are theoretically
available that finesse the seeming contradiction between sex equality
and cultural attachment, in practice these two may still be counter-
posed. The judge and the deliberative democrat provide us with two
models for addressing dilemmas of gender and culture. But if much
of the complexity lies in assessing the impact of particular claims in
particular historical contexts, we may have to move beyond these
two figures to include the perspective of the political activist.

I approach this in three stages. In the first section, I take issue with
the notion of intractable value conflict, arguing that the conflicts
become more open to (at least theoretical) resolution when framed
within a common rubric of equality, and that this enables us to move
beyond what might otherwise seem incommensurable claims. The
theoretical argument is reinforced by an empirical claim about the
modesty of most of the policies practised in the name of multiculturalism, particularly in the multicultural societies that have been formed
by more recent large-scale migration. In the second section, I question
the tendency to separate gender from culture. This tendency is most
marked when sex equality is set up as a competing value to cultural
integrity, and the adjudicator has to decide which one matters most;
but it is also at issue under a common rubric of equality, which too
readily generates a notion of competing equality claims. In the third
section, I briefly consider three illustrations: two much discussed in
the literature and a third arising from recent British debates. None
of them raises hugely complex questions about justice. In varying

degrees, however, they all raise difficult questions of political action, and part of that difficulty is contextual. From the perspective of the judge, the task is to determine which principles of justice to follow. From the perspective of the democrat, this involves a more dialogic process, but still one that should ultimately generate normative agreement. From the perspective of the political activist, the question of what is ethically just cannot be so easily detached from judgements about the effects of one's actions, and, where there is reason to think that these will be at odds with the original intentions, it can be an abdication of political responsibility not to take this into account. In my view, it is in this, rather than 'deep disagreement', that many of the dilemmas of multiculturalism lie.

Against intractable value conflict

The first point is that the tensions within the politics of minority rights become more amenable to settlement when we take equality as the defining concern. The literature on multiculturalism is not always helpful here, for while cultural diversity claims typically invoke some notion of equality (as in the equal right to respect, or the equal requirement for a meaningful cultural context), the emphasis has often been on the need for recognition. When multiculturalism is theorized primarily as a way of meeting claims for cultural recognition, it can indeed be difficult to address conflicts between a group's right to cultural autonomy or recognition and a sub-group's right to equality. Failing some a-priori commitment to either sex equality or cultural recognition, there seems no obvious way of resolving the tension.

The problem changes shape, however, if we think of multiculturalism as a way of meeting legitimate equality claims. Multicultural policies are still a pressing objective, necessary to address the unequal treatment of minority cultural groups and the 'culture-racism' to which so many are exposed. If, however, the object is to promote equality, then an inequality of women enters on the same terrain. This echoes a similar point made by Jacob Levy, who reconfigures multiculturalism as a way of redressing cruelty and violence, and argues that there would not be the same 'moral difficulty' (he acknowledges continuing practical difficulties) in restraining internal practices of cruelty against women if multiculturalism were itself grounded in the need to avoid cruelty.[7] By the same token, there would not be the same moral difficulty in challenging an inegalitarian treatment of women if the whole point of multiculturalism were to challenge the unequal treatment of minority groups. The treatment of women figures more centrally in a discourse of either equality or cruelty than in one that revolves around the recognition of cultural groups.

My own position is that egalitarians should be committed to both sex equality and at least some version of multiculturalism. That they should be committed to equality between women and men can probably pass without further comment, though it is worth noting that self-professed egalitarians adopt very different positions on what this equality entails. In the case of multiculturalism, there is not even the initial consensus: there are egalitarians who object to what they see as its social divisiveness and cultural relativism, and pragmatic supporters who see it as a way of pre-empting political friction rather than anything to do with equality per se. Many of the difficulties here arise from problematic claims about 'cultural equality': problematic both in treating 'cultures' as distinct and separate entities, and in the suggestion that all cultural practices are of equal moral worth. If we steer clear, however, of this more dubious terrain, it is possible to establish a pretty strong connection between egalitarianism and at least some version of multiculturalism. In the multiethnic, multireligious, multicultural societies that characterize this age of global migration, the idea that access to resources, occupations or political voice should be conditional on adopting what one (usually historically dominant) group has deemed the appropriate practices and values is self-evidently coercive. It is a form of coercion, moreover, that actively asserts the superiority of one set of cultural beliefs and practices over all others, or – perhaps more commonly – simply fails to notice that these beliefs and practices are imbued with the cultural traditions of a dominant or majority group. Principles of non-discrimination alone suggest that societies need to revisit their legislative codes and administrative practices to determine which of these operates as a means of cultural domination. Principles of political equality additionally suggest that they should address taken-for-granted assumptions about who can speak and in what terms. The impetus towards multiculturalism arises from a perception of indefensible inequalities that have become associated with cultural membership, and a suspicion that numerical majorities have imposed their own cultural values under the guise of what they take to be universal norms. It also arises – and this has become particularly important in recent years – from a perception of the 'culture-racism' that increasingly substitutes for the crudities of biological racism, and reframes now-discredited notions of biological superiority in a less overtly racist discourse about practices that are 'backward' or 'foreign'.

If equality is the key value underpinning initiatives on multiculturalism, it will continue to be cause for gloom if policies designed to
redress the disadvantages of a cultural minority backfire on the
women within it, but hardly an occasion for cross-cultural despair.
Indeed, in many ways, the deliberative apparatus proposed by political theorists for dealing with troubled questions of cultural pluralism
seems unnecessarily large for the task. Commenting on a *Report on
the Future of Multi-Ethnic Britain* – the work of a commission
chaired by Bhikhu Parekh, and significantly influenced by his vision
of inter-cultural dialogue – Brian Barry notes that virtually all the
recommendations can be justified by reference to principles of non-
discrimination. There was, in his view, no need to muddy the waters
by a dubious accretion of cultural pluralism: 'the Report gives hos-
tages to fortune by propounding a theory of multiculturalism as
pluralism that is almost entirely dispensable as a support for its specific recommendations'.[8] Or consider an example offered by Monique
Deveaux of the potentially deep clash of values within culturally
plural societies: the bid for state funding for Islamic schools in the
UK.[9] She presents this as at odds with liberal sensibilities because
children educated in such schools would be discouraged from taking
up lifestyles at odds with Islam, and proposes inclusive procedures
of democratic dialogue as a way of dealing with these potentially
incommensurate moral and social beliefs. Yet this question was
largely resolved by reference to principles of equity, for in a country
already practising state funding for religious schools (and funding
large numbers of Catholic and Anglican schools), principles of non-
discrimination alone required the extension of state-aided status to a
wider range of denominations. It was hardly necessary to invoke the
additional apparatus of inter-cultural dialogue to reach this conclusion; indeed, it might be argued that making such dialogue a pre-
condition for policy change constitutes Islam as intrinsically more
sexist and coercive than the Christian religions.

Deep value conflict is more rare than is sometimes suggested, and
not much in evidence in most of the policies associated with multiculturalism, which fall largely into the categories of extensions,
exemptions and autonomy. Some policies seek to extend to other
cultural groups 'privileges' previously enjoyed only by members of
the majority or dominant culture. The object, in other words, is to
redress a previous bias – sometimes deliberate, sometimes just
unthinking – and ensure more equitable treatment. Extending a principle of state support for denominational schools to include religions
associated with more recent migrants would be one obvious example
of this. Other initiatives seek exemptions for members of particular

cultural groups from requirements that are legally binding on other citizens, the usual justification being that conformity requires a greater sacrifice of cultural or religious values for some groups than others. The equality at issue is usually the equal freedom to pursue one's religion, though it may also be that, failing the exemption, a cultural group would be discriminated against in its pursuit of employment. Exemptions are, on the face of it, more troubling to notions of citizen equality than extending to other groups privileges previously enjoyed only by one – except that most of the current examples relate to relatively innocuous matters of food and dress. While these give a public validity to claims about cultural identity, and could as a result strengthen the power of religious and cultural leaders over dissident members of the cultural group, the immediate implications for gender equality are pretty mild.

Autonomy has been a rarer policy, mainly arising as part of a historical settlement with indigenous peoples, under colonial practices of indirect rule, or in countries where potentially hostile communities would actively resist incorporation into a single legislative norm. In these cases, cultural communities retain authority in the regulation of certain aspects of property or family affairs, and citizens may come under different jurisdictions depending on their religious or cultural attachments. This is the category that has been thought to throw up the hardest cases, for the resulting regulations may well put women at a disadvantage in relation to men, thereby raising the prospect of external intervention to secure more equitable treatment. Yet, even here, the disagreement is hardly a matter of deep value conflict, rooted in incommensurable traditions and beliefs, for what is at stake is which group has the power to decide. The arguments are typically conducted in a shared language of self-government. Do indigenous minorities, for example, have the right to determine for themselves their own practices in relation to inheritance? Do religious authorities have the right to regulate their own members' marital affairs? Does the larger state have the authority to impose the practices it regards as the best? There is undoubtedly disagreement on such issues, but the substance of the argument is power.

Gender versus culture:
not a matter of competing equality claims

Moving towards a common rubric of equality undercuts some of the more tendentious claims about deep value conflict, and provides a promising guide in situations where the needs of the larger and the smaller minority threaten to collide. It is tempting, at this point, to adopt a language of competing equality claims: to say that multiculturalism addresses the inequalities experienced by cultural minorities, and feminism the inequalities experienced by women; that both these projects draw on a shared commitment to equality; and that the two concerns must therefore be balanced in circumstances where they appear to collide. Neither, in other words, 'trumps' the other, and since both are driven by the same underlying commitment, the promotion of the first must not be at the expense of the second.

The partial truth in this is that both sex equality and multiculturalism are driven by questions of equality, but it does not, I believe, help to set them up as competing equality claims. Such a formulation generates an understanding of gender and culture as two distinct systems. This encourages us to think there is a pristine set of 'cultural' claims that then have to be modified by gender concerns. Culture is thereby degendered, and one of the central themes of feminist scholarship since the early 1990s is that when something is degendered, a masculine interpretation usually rushes in to fill the vacuum. If this insight is correct, then setting up culture as a separate system (defining our first minority group), whose claims we subsequently balance by considerations of women's equality (our second minority group), is likely to reinforce precisely those patriarchal interpretations of cultural traditions and values that feminists have been criticizing. The dual systems approach does not, of course, commit us to condoning all these traditions, for we are then supposed to weigh up their claims against the claims of sex equality. But it gives an added authenticity to the more conservative representations of culture – and, to that extent, already concedes more than it should.

One of the key challenges for any discussion of culture is to avoid what Uma Narayan has termed the 'package picture of cultures': the presumption that cultures exist as neatly wrapped packages, sealed off from one another, and identifiable by core values and practices that mark them out from all others.[10] The package picture is highly congenial to cultural spokesmen – usually men – who want to claim particular practices as definitive of their culture, and is all too often adopted by Western liberals whose anxieties about cultural imperialism lead them to exaggerate the 'otherness' of cultures they see as different from their own. Yet, in a process Narayan terms 'selective labelling', certain changes in values and practices are designated as consonant with cultural preservation while others are treated as threatening the entire survival of the culture. Culture can also be drafted in to explain behaviour more accurately described as authoritarian parenting or domestic violence: this is one of the perennial risks in legal defences that refer to religious or cultural beliefs to explain or mitigate a defendant's behaviour. Feminists have criticized the use of culture in the courts to excuse violence against women, but the point is not just that something called cultural identity has sometimes been allowed to take precedence over ensuring women's equality or safety. In many cases, the claim that an action was culturally driven also does deep disservice to other members of that cultural community, whose beliefs and practices are being misrepresented to explain behaviour they would never support.

Caution is always necessary in dealing with invocations of culture, for this is a term that lends itself readily to cultural essentialism, cultural reification and the dissemination of cultural stereotypes. The balancing of 'cultural' against 'gender' concerns should also be treated with caution, for such an approach encourages us to accept a pristine definition of culture, which we only then interrogate by reference to women's equality concerns. Meanwhile, setting up gender as distinct from culture encourages the belief that there is a culture-neutral set of values that provides us with the principles for equality between women and men. And where do we find these? Usually in the dominant, therefore less visible culture, which has become such a taken-for-granted background that its members no longer think of themselves as sharing any particular cultural traditions or beliefs.

The selective invocation of culture leads to an over-culturation of those marked by a minority ethnicity or religion – a tendency to treat their every characteristic or behaviour as an expression of their culture – but also to an under-culturation of those associated with the dominant group.[11] The hyper-visibility of culture for one group is then linked to an invisibility of culture for another: they have cultural traditions, while I have moral values. Again, the analytic separation of gender from culture makes it harder to avoid this trap. When gender is stripped of its cultural context, the less visible – because dominant – culture rushes in to fill the vacuum, and we then have a culturally informed interpretation of sex equality that presents itself as above all culture. Black feminists used to say of an earlier theorization of gender and race that it gave the impression that all the women were white and all the blacks were male. Similar problems arise when we set up gender and culture as separate concerns. The further difficulty with the discourse of competing equality claims – and here I return to my central argument – is that this formulation misrepresents what are often political and strategic questions as more fundamental conflicts of justice. Though the notion of competing claims helpfully provides us with a common measure of equality through which to address dilemmas of cultural pluralism, it does so in a way that reinforces the more conservative (because pre-gendered) representations of minority cultures, and in the process heightens the differences between one culture and another. This exaggerates the dilemmas that arise where the practices of multiculturalism fall into the rather modest categories of extension or exemption, and where there may be relatively few areas of principled disagreement. It also, I think, exaggerates those that arise in countries where there has been a significant devolution of power to cultural or religious groups. But in defining cultural problems as primarily conflicts of value, the literature also *under-estimates* the more contextual political dilemmas. It is in these contextual dilemmas that many of the problems lie.

Political dilemmas

The first example revolves around the conflict that has arisen between recognizing the self-government rights of indigenous minorities and ensuring the equal status of their men and women members. In many parts of the world, Aboriginal peoples were thrust into a quasi-colonial system of native reserves or reservations. These worked as a kind of apartheid, but, within their much-circumscribed limits, usually provided Aboriginal communities with some self-government powers. In both Canada and the USA, the membership rules governing these communities have sometimes been overtly sexist, most typically in disenfranchising the women (and their descendants) who married outside the group but not the men who did so. Women have sometimes challenged this by reference to a wider federal or international authority, and have then found themselves in conflict with the self-government claims of their group. This has been particularly problematic for those who support both claims.

Legislation in Canada in 1985 reversed the membership discrimination, to the dismay of some band councils, who not only felt themselves ill equipped to provide for those who now applied to be reinstated as full-status Indians, but also regarded the change in membership rules as an illegitimate intervention in internal affairs. This linked to the larger issue of whether Indian councils should be bound by the sex equality provisions of the 1982 Charter of Rights and Freedoms, which had proved an important instrument for securing women's rights. Matters came to a head in 1992 with the referendum on the Charlottetown Accord. The Accord contained a strong statement recognizing the 'inherent right to self-government', and, while the precise implications of this were left unclear, it was explicitly stated that self-government would include the power to suspend aspects of the Charter. At this point, two principles seemed on collision course. The rights of the larger minority could be recognized in the right to self-government; or the rights of the minority within the minority could be recognized through the Charter of Rights and Freedoms. How were these competing and seemingly irreconcilable claims to be resolved?

As is often the case, this way of posing the issue exaggerates the essential conflict. Monique Deveaux has shown that many of the women involved argued *both* for a constitutional recognition of the right to self-government *and* for an assurance that this would not override their federally guaranteed equality rights.[12] Self-government, in their view, did not mean being relieved of all wider obligations in national and international law, and certainly did not mean being relieved of the obligation to treat men and women as equals. And this was not just muddled thinking, or trying to have things both ways, for only a very strict interpretation of sovereignty (of the kind implied by those who view UK membership of the European Union as destroying the sovereignty of the nation state) would see it as at odds with any wider restrictions. Indeed, in a world where international conventions of human rights increasingly set limits to national sovereignty, it seems anachronistic to insist that being 'a government' means retaining the authority to determine all aspects of internal affairs. The judicial approach to minority rights thrives on either/or choices that require careful adjudication. In this instance, there was no such stark alternative.

Or rather, there was no such stark alternative in principle, but, at the moment of the referendum, this finessing of self-government with sex equality was not the choice on offer. Aboriginal women had to choose between supporting (somewhat unspecified) powers of self-government or insisting on sex equality rights, and, if they chose the latter, there was a good chance that the referendum would fail. In the event, this was exactly what occurred. Their leaders, most notably the Native Women's Association of Canada (NWAC), were highly critical of an agreement that had been drawn up without their involvement, and challenged a version of self-government that implied an erosion of women's rights; the Accord was defeated (interestingly, it was rejected by two-thirds of native peoples living on reserves);

and the much-publicized division between native women's groups and other Aboriginal leaders was held partly responsible for the defeat.

At a theoretical level, there was no need for this conflict: no reason why self-government could not be combined with an assurance of sex equality rights. But in the political context of the early 1990s – and the longer historical context of dispossession and denial – there must have been much agonizing on whether joining battle on the sex equality front was going to undermine initiatives towards fuller self-government. Some people certainly felt that the position adopted by the NWAC bolstered general opposition to any kind of Accord. In her reading of events, Deveaux notes that the later Commission on Aboriginal Peoples recommended increased self-government rights, but now attached to this a much stronger insistence that native communities should not use discretionary powers to suspend women's rights. She suggested, that is, that the First Nations might soon get both self-government *and* sexual equality. A more gloomy reading might say that, in the conflict between the two, substantive self-government had had its day. Let me stress here: I am not suggesting that native women should have set aside their equality concerns in order to ensure a smoother passage to self-government. I am just pointing out the difficult choices posed by political context, even when the principles may seem relatively clear.

Similar difficulties arise when denouncing practices of sexual discrimination becomes a vehicle for attacking a minority group. This was a key issue in the *Shah Bano* case in India, which revolved around the inequitable treatment of women under systems of personal law, but became bound up with tensions between Hindu majority and Muslim minority. The post-partition settlement in India retained many of the features of British indirect rule. Instead of a uniform civil code governing all matters of marriage and succession, four religious communities (Hindu, Muslim, Christian and Parsi) were accorded their own separate systems of personal law; other groups, like Buddhists, Sikhs and Jains, were subsumed under Hindu law; there was also provision for people to opt for a secular code. Though all the personal law systems discriminate in some way against women, some are more sexually egalitarian than others. Polygamy is permitted, for example, under the legislation governing Muslim marriages, but was eventually prohibited under the Hindu code; and one recurrent problem for Muslim women is the derisory divorce settlements they have been awarded under usually very conservative interpretations of Islamic personal law.

Up until 1986, their main recourse was to the Criminal Procedure Code, which forbids a man of adequate means to leave close relatives in a state of destitution. Since this code applied to all, a number of Muslim women had successfully appealed to it to establish claims to maintenance on divorce. Shah Bano, unilaterally divorced after forty-three years, and left with little more than the dowry payment she originally brought to the marriage, took her case to the Supreme Court in 1985, where she was awarded a monthly maintenance payment. But the Chief Justice took the opportunity to single out Muslim men and the Islamic system as almost uniquely unjust to women, and said it was about time India moved to a uniform civil code. Not surprisingly, this was interpreted by Muslim religious leaders as part of a growing pattern of Hindu supremacy. After the very public campaign against this ruling, the Government introduced in 1986 the misleadingly titled Muslim Women's (Protection of Rights On Divorce) Act, which deprived Muslim women – and only Muslim women – of the right to claim maintenance under the Criminal Procedure Code. In one of the sadder aspects of the case, Shah Bano capitulated to what must have been almost unbearable pressure from the leaders of her community, renounced her claims to maintenance, and declared her full support for the operation of Islamic personal law.

The Muslim Women's Act seems to me thoroughly indefensible, as does a system of personal law that permitted the unilateral divorce of a wife of forty-three years and allowed her virtually no claim on the family assets. But, against the background of the very fraught relations between Hindus and Muslims, and the heavily disadvantaged position of the Muslim minority, it was not just a question of what is right and wrong, but how best to intervene in a context where sex equality issues were being employed to promote hatred between different communities. Political context matters, and it proved hard in the Indian context to detach the case for a uniform civil code from its association with Hindu attacks on the so-called 'special privileges' (polygyny, lesser maintenance obligations) of the Muslim minority. As groups jostle to establish their moral superiority, issues relating to sex equality are often harnessed to more devious ends, and those whose own practices bear little scrutiny may still revel in their claim to be better in their treatment of women. The Committee on the Status of Women in India reported in 1975 that, despite being banned for Hindus and legal for Muslims, the incidence of polygyny was actually higher among Hindu than Muslim men (5.8 per cent of the former, 5.7 per cent of the latter). One would never guess at this similarity from some of the denunciations of Islamic law.

Various attempts to challenge the constitutionality of the Muslim Women's Act – on the grounds that it discriminates against Muslim women – have so far failed, though a key Supreme Court judgment in 2001 significantly improved the level of maintenance for divorced Muslim women through its reinterpretation of the Act.[13] It remains, however, the case that Muslim women are uniquely denied recourse to the secular provisions of the Criminal Procedure Code. Before the Shah Bano case, Indian feminists tended to favour a secular solution and uniform civil code, but virtually none now argues for state imposition of a civil code, the main options being either reform from within of the various personal law systems, or a state-sponsored civil code operating alongside personal law. The shift in this direction was not entirely driven by strategic considerations. As Rajeswari Sunder Rajan notes, there was also concern that the implicit secularism of the mainstream women's movement pays too little attention to the differences among women that derive from their religious identities, and the possibly greater importance of these identities to lower-caste women.[14] But while there continues to be enormous disagreement among feminists on the best way of reforming personal law, the fact remains that there is no deep disagreement on substantive issues. For Indian feminists, this is not so much a normative debate as one inextricably embedded in a particular political context.

The same complex of political and contextual dilemmas characterizes my third example: initiatives in Britain to address the problem of forced marriage, and the difficulties of disentangling these from association with a potentially racist immigration debate.[15] In South Asian families – Hindu, Sikh and Muslim – parents, and sometimes some other family elder, have commonly played a role in the selection of marriage partners for their children, often promoting marriages between first cousins or between uncle and niece. The tradition is in decline amongst those living in Britain, and, while a majority still consult their parents, most young Hindus and Sikhs now say they make the final decision themselves. Arranged marriages are also declining among those of Pakistani and Bangladeshi origin, 95 per cent of whom are Muslim, though, in a 1995 survey, a majority even of the under-35s still reported that their parents made the decision.[16] The government line is that arranged marriage is an entirely legitimate cultural variation, but there has been growing concern over the 1–4,000 young people thought to be forced into marriages each year, and considerable government activity since 1999 to tackle this problem.

This is not on the face of it an issue that throws up particularly vexed questions of cultural accommodation. No one is suggesting that the state should defer to some cherished minority custom of forcing young girls into marriages against their will. None of the spokesmen of the South Asian communities claims *forced* – as opposed to arranged – marriage as part of their cultural or religious heritage. No one suggests that laws against rape, child abuse, abduction or false imprisonment should be suspended in deference to 'cultural' practice. The difficulty, rather, is that the initiative on forced marriage has become entangled with immigration issues, with the distinction between arranged and forced marriage superimposed on the very different distinction between marrying someone from Britain or from overseas.

Some arranged marriages involve partners from overseas; and some of the most dramatic examples of forced marriage involve young people being tricked into travelling to Bangladesh or Pakistan, only then to discover that a marriage has been arranged. Whether consensual or coerced, these transcontinental marriages will usually result in the spouse's application for entry to Britain, and, for some commentators, the distinction between arranged and forced then becomes irrelevant, for any marriage between a British citizen and a spouse from the Indian sub-continent is regarded as 'bogus', entered into for purposes of migration. There has been a long history in the UK of immigration officials subjecting marriages with spouses from the Indian sub-continent to close and suspicious scrutiny. This practice was indeed officially sanctioned under the now-repealed 'primary purpose' rule, which gave entry clearance officers the power to decide whether a marriage was entered into primarily for the purpose of migration to the UK. There is no known 'primary purpose' case involving two white spouses; and the rule was widely perceived as a way of restricting the number of black and Asian people entering the country. For many Britons of South Asian origin, the government's new zeal for addressing the incidence of forced marriage looked suspiciously like a back-door attempt to restore this rule. Indeed, when the Foreign and Commonwealth Office sponsored research into perceptions of forced marriage in Britain's Bangladeshi and Pakistani communities, it uncovered widespread suspicion (though primarily among middle-aged and older men) that the government's preoccupation with this issue reflected racist and Islamophobic intentions: 'Immigration control was considered to be the authorities' main aim and the research was seen as a veiled assault on arranged marriages.'[17]

The (mainly Asian) women's groups that have campaigned to expose the incidence of forced marriage have been more unambiguous in supporting strong public action on this issue, but they, too, have registered concern about the way initiatives to tackle the undoubted harm of forced marriage became caught up in a potentially racist immigration debate. It is troubling, for example, that all the major developments in relation to forced marriage have focused on what is termed the 'overseas dimension'; and that initiatives in recent years have included raising the age of entry for spouses from outside the European Union above the prevailing age of marriage within the UK. The merging of sex equality with immigration issues makes for difficult political terrain, so while women's groups mostly welcomed the government's belated recognition of the problem of forced marriage, their work on this issue has been repeatedly framed by worries about playing into the anti-immigration camp. Enabling women to escape the threat or reality of a forced marriage remains the overwhelming priority, but when the defence of women's rights threatens to resuscitate the now discredited primary purpose rule, this is inevitably a source of concern.

Those who regard the minorities within minorities dilemma as throwing up 'hard cases' of value disagreement may object that I have considered the above examples from the perspective of political activists, thus from the perspective of those who already share a similar moral universe, and have already worked out (to their own satisfaction, at least) their stance on the normative concerns. But this is precisely my point. Even when then there is no deep disagreement, there are still enormously complex dilemmas; and many of these arise because discourses of women's rights can be deployed to serve such different ends. In each of the above examples, campaigners face dilemmas of political context. They are seeking to ensure that women's equality is not sacrificed to the claims of expediency or traditional culture, but to ensure at the same time that these equality claims are not invoked as part of a project of cultural supremacy or a form of immigration control.

The cases do not, on the whole, illustrate a conflict between the rights of a minority group and the rights of a sub-group within it. Such a formulation presumes in advance that something called 'culture' dictates inequality between the sexes, and attributes any incidence of women's subordination to cultural values and traditions. This is a risky assumption: it is not 'culture' that dictates the unequal treatment of women, but particular interpretations of cultural tradition, sometimes quite deliberately invoked so as to block women's equality claims. The point, to reiterate, is that the value conflict – between the values of sex equality and the values of particular cultural traditions – is often overstated. It is not that there is a fundamental conflict between two equality claims, or that societies must devise complex adjudication procedures or new practices of democratic deliberation in order to balance these out. The more pressing problem, in many cases, is that sex equality claims are already implicated in other discourses – anti-immigrant, anti-Muslim, anti-indigenous peoples – that egalitarians will want to avoid.

Political theorists tend to get stuck on the normative issues: which principles of justice? Which principles of adjudication? How to determine what is right and wrong? The point I have stressed is that many of the (very real) dilemmas signposted by the phrase 'minorities within minorities' arise somewhere else in the chain. Often enough, the most pressing issue is how to formulate strong policies for sex equality that do not feed on and feed into cultural stereotypes, and how to reframe discourses of sex equality so as to detach them from projects of cultural or racial superiority. The key problems, to put it another way, may be those that arise from the perspective of the political activist rather than that of the constitutional lawyer, or even the deliberative democrat. It is these problems of political action that represent the real challenge for those committed to both multiculturalism and sex equality.

4

What is 'culture'?

'Culture', as Raymond Williams famously said, 'is ordinary',[1] part of the process through which any social organization develops and reproduces itself. Williams understood the term as referring to the shared meanings transmitted from one generation to another. As a literary critic, he was especially keen to stress that culture is not just transmitted, but debated and amended in ways that express the creativity of the human mind. In this understanding of the term, culture is both ubiquitous and in a continual process of change.

Anthropologists have also stressed the ubiquity of culture, though they have been more pre-occupied with questions of cross-cultural interpretation, and the difficulties of understanding what people are doing when they inhabit a culture very different from one's own. This can lend itself to exoticism – the presumption that the study of culture is the study of strange peoples pursuing strange practices in lands far away – but there is no reason, in principle, why it should do so. Indeed, for much of the twentieth century, anthropologists were the ones insisting that all peoples have their own complex and internally coherent cultures, thus providing, as Etienne Balibar puts it, 'the humanist and cosmopolitan anti-racism of the post-war period with most of its arguments'.[2] Typically, this was achieved through the study of remote cultural groups, whose initially puzzling practices and beliefs were then shown to have a coherence and rationality of their own. But some of the most interesting work in contemporary anthropology also turns the spotlight back on the Western countries whose colonial exploits so shaped the discipline, and applies the methods of anthropology to the metropolis itself. Culture, again, appears as an attribute of all societies. The study of culture is not a matter of exotic others. It is also the study of one's own society or group.

As is now widely noted, normative political theory has tended to employ culture in a more restrictive way.[3] Political theorists are consumed by questions of justice, equality and autonomy, and, in a period dominated by the discourse of human rights, have been particularly preoccupied by what rights, if any, can be claimed by minority groups. Culture then enters the field of investigation not so much as difference (how to understand the meaning of practices across different cultures?) but as inequality (how to determine what counts as just treatment of minority groups?). It was the recognition of unequal power relations between majority and minority groups, and the perception that states may unfairly disadvantage citizens from minority cultural groups when they impose a unitary political and legal framework, that gave the impetus to recent debates about multiculturalism. Political theorists are – to their credit – political. They think about inequality and power.

But this means that culture crossed their horizon already attached to distinctions between majority and minority, and already linked to territorial or legal claims. Will Kymlicka is barely a paragraph into *Multicultural Citizenship* before noting that '[m]inorities and majorities increasingly clash over such issues as language rights, regional autonomy, political representation, education curriculum, land claims, immigration and naturalization policy, even national symbols, such as the choice of national anthem or public holidays'.[4] These are the clashes he seeks to resolve, hence (I would suggest) his decision to employ 'culture' as virtually synonymous with nation or people, referring to 'an intergenerational community, more or less institutionally complete, occupying a given territory or homeland, sharing a distinct language and history'.[5] The definition conjures up a group of considerable solidity. It has its own institutions, its own territories, its own language and history, and, by implication, its own potentially extensive claims on the loyalty of its members. We will not be surprised to learn that such groups are often in conflict with each other. In similar fashion, Ayelet Shachar adopts the term *nomoi* community to refer to a group that has 'a comprehensive and distinguishable worldview that extends to creating a law for the community'.[6] The groups that interest Shachar – those whose claims to accommodation she wants to consider and assess – are ones that are already staking extensive claims. They are distinguished not just by particular systems of meaning, or specific codes of conduct that teach their members what is considered appropriate or rude behaviour. These are groups that seek to regulate through law the behaviour of community members.

In the political theorist's understanding of culture, 'cultural group' then becomes associated with a quasi-legal entity that has historically enjoyed, or is now claiming, jurisdiction over its members. This solidifies the group into something very substantial. The group is presumed, moreover, to play a large role in the loyalties of its members; hence the emphasis, from Charles Taylor onwards, on the responsibility states have to extend due respect and recognition to cultures. Taylor has linked this to a strong sense of what distinguishes one group from another: 'with the politics of difference', he argues, 'what we are being asked to recognise is the unique identity of the individual or group, their distinctness from everyone else'.[7] Sustaining that distinctness becomes a large part of what cultural politics is about. People's loyalty to their group does not necessarily displace loyalty to a larger national community (Kymlicka and Taylor tend to be rather reassuring on this score), but with distinctness so strongly emphasized, there is a tendency to see group identities as intrinsically oppositional.

In Jacob Levy's characterization of ethnocultural identities, for example, cultural belonging is linked to a demarcation between strangers and kin:

> Persons identify and empathize more easily with those with whom they have more in common than with those with whom they have less. They rally around their fellow religionists; they seek the familiar comforts of native speakers of their native languages; they support those they see as kin against those they see as strangers. They seek places that feel like home, and seek to protect those places; they are raised in particular cultures, with particular sets of knowledge, norms and traditions, which come to seem normal and enduring. These feelings, repeated and generalized, help give rise to a world of ethnic, cultural and national loyalty, and also a world of enduring ethnic, cultural, and national variety.[8]

This is a pretty bounded conception of culture, presuming not only a preference for, but also a clear sense of, who counts as your kin. It makes culture, almost by definition, oppositional: 'my' culture means 'not yours'. To have a culture is to find your ways of doing things more natural than any other, and to feel greater allegiance to those you regard as your own.

These tendencies – reserving the term cultural group for quasi-legal entities, thinking of the 'problem' of culture as intrinsically bound up with the status of minority groups, and associating cultural belonging with potentially exclusionary loyalties – reflect the political theorist's awareness of inequality and conflict, and are not in themselves bad things. The downside is an overly solid representation of the cultural group, and this has had a number of unfortunate consequences. The first is that theorists of multiculturalism focus on conflicts between majority and minority groups but do not sufficiently consider conflicts (for example, by gender, age or class) within each group. They take the 'group' as more of an entity than it really is, and play down internal tensions. I will not dwell on this aspect, for it is has by now been widely criticized, most notably in the feminism versus multiculturalism debates. A substantial feminist literature extends the now familiar critique of gender essentialism to make similar charges against 'cultural essentialism';[9] and even those feminists said to be guilty of this cultural essentialism – Susan Moller Okin, for example – engage in a deconstruction of culture, if only in noting that the self-styled spokesmen of a cultural community cannot be taken as speaking for the women in 'their' group. Pretty much all feminist writing on multiculturalism starts with a warning against the tendency to take the cultural 'group' as more unified and homogeneous than it really is. The way cultural reification can obscure internal differentiation by age, gender, sexuality or class has by now been widely aired.

I focus here on two other consequences of the overly solid depiction of the cultural group. The first is that culture comes to be seen as the major source of people's identity, and major determinant of their actions and behaviour. The second – almost a direct result of the first – is that culture comes to be seen as primarily associated with non-Western or minority cultural groups. As the political case for multiculturalism comes to rest, in part, on the importance people attach to their cultural identities, the hold that 'culture' exerts over people is highlighted and exaggerated, and culture is thereby exoticized. Culture comes to be represented as something of enormous importance to the individual. It is treated as more important to our sense of ourselves than our sex or our class, and is attributed far more explanatory value. But the greater the importance attached to cultural belonging, the more likely it is that culture will be seen as something that matters to others, not me, for culture is, in most people's lives, pretty 'ordinary'. It is such a taken-for-granted background that we only become aware of the norms and assumptions that give meaning to our actions when we are confronted with cultures very different from our own. (This was the key insight of the ethno-methodologist,

who asks us to disrupt taken-for-granted rules of conduct in order
to bring them into sharper focus.)

Culture tends, moreover, to be least visible to those in a hegemonic
culture, many of whom will readily acknowledge the influence of
class or gender on their attitudes and behaviour, but rarely cite
'culture' as explaining why they act the way they do. I am not convinced that culture is lived in such a different way by those who find
themselves in a minority. But the experience of being in a minority
makes people more conscious of the distinctiveness of their culture,
while the sense of being pressured to conform to majority norms
sometimes makes people more committed to sustaining their distinctiveness. Culture also operates as a resource in mobilizing against
majority dominance. With all this, it is hardly surprising if individuals
occupying a minority position more commonly refer to their culture
as a defining part of their identity and being.[10]

These different ways of living a hegemonic and non-hegemonic
culture help sustain the notion that 'culture' – in the sense of cultural
traditions, practices or beliefs – is primarily a feature of non-Western
or minority cultural groups. In *Dislocating Cultures*, Uma Narayan
conjures up an imaginary Indian journalist who is trying to write an
analysis of the way 'American culture' kills women, a book that will
do for domestic violence in the USA what analyses of 'Hindu tradition' have done for dowry-murder in India. She concludes that this
can only remain 'an imaginary chapter in an improbable book', for
'while Indian women repeatedly suffer "death by culture" in a range
of scholarly and popular works, even as the elements of "culture"
proffered do little to explain their deaths, American women seem
relatively immune to such analyses of "death or injury by culture"
even as they are victimized by the fairly distinctively American phenomenon of wide-spread gun-related violence'.[11] The hard work of
the anthropologists has not, it seems, borne fruit. Despite their best
efforts, people seem unwilling to recognize that all groups have their
cultural practices, expectations and traditions, and that each of us
lives within a web of cultural references and meanings.

In the political theory of multiculturalism, this tendency to associate cultural tradition with minority cultural tradition is compounded
by the very way the argument for multicultural policies has been
pursued, for if the case for multiculturalism rests on the importance
people attach to their cultural identities and belonging, it rests on
something that is not widely experienced by the average political
theorist. The academics who generate most of the writing on this
topic live in an atmosphere of geographic and intellectual mobility.

However strongly they may defend the 'right to culture', they are likely to be less culturally embedded than those they write about. In popular thinking, culture has become almost synonymous with minority or non-Western culture. Much the same has happened in normative political theory.

Exaggerating the significance of culture

In the literature on multiculturalism, there is by now a well-developed understanding of two pitfalls that can beset us in considering tensions between gender equality and cultural diversity. We know it is danger-ous to invoke something called culture as justifying or excusing harms to women, for we know that the cultural brokers who take on the role of interpretation may be a narrowly unrepresentative elite, employing what they claim to be the unbreakable traditions of their culture to reinforce the subordination of women. We also know – from the other side – that it can be problematic simply to invoke the rights of women against the claims of cultural groups. This can leave women with an unhappy choice between their rights or their culture, and seems to ignore the inequalities between majority and minority groups that first gave the impetus to debates on multiculturalism. In representing some cultures as more sexist than others, it can also give a perverse legitimacy to xenophobic and racist attacks. The further problem I focus on here is the tendency to make 'culture' more important than it is in explaining events in non-Western or minority cultures, whilst minimizing its significance elsewhere.

Some of the most disturbing illustrations arise in relation to cul-tural defence, discussed in more detail later in this volume, though it is worth noting that defendants invoking the norms and practices of their culture in a criminal defence have not got much of a hearing in courts across North America and Europe. The most comprehensive survey to date reports that judges commonly refuse to hear expert witnesses testifying about cultural context, declaring this irrelevant to the case at hand; and concludes that 'the preponderance of the data belies the commitment of liberal democracies to the value of cultural diversity'.[12] In a search of cases in the English courts, I have identified only one where a defendant successfully invoked his reli-gious and cultural beliefs as part of a plea of provocation: the case of Shabir Hussain, who drove into and reversed his car over his sister-in-law while she was waiting on a pavement for her lover, but was convicted of the lesser offence of manslaughter and sentenced to six and a half years in prison. That there are any such cases is deeply troubling. But, in my reading, the larger issue for the coming years will not be the mitigating use of culture (leading to reduced sentences) but its explanatory role. Courts will, on the whole, reject what they see as an illegitimate use of culture to justify a more lenient treatment of minority ethnic defendants in cases involving violence against the person. They may, nonetheless, accept and reproduce the idea that these defendants were 'driven' by their culture. In doing so, they will represent members of minority and/or non-Western cultures as less than autonomous beings.

When culture becomes the catch-all explanation for everything that goes awry in non-Western societies or minority cultural groups, while remaining an invisible force elsewhere, something has gone wrong with the use of the term. The killing of those one is supposedly closest to is not a minority practice. Or rather, it is a minority practice, in that most people do not kill their daughters or sisters or wives, but it is by no means a peculiarity of minority cultural groups. As I note in chapter 6, so-called honour crimes compare with a much larger category of cases where male violence has been rendered explicable without any reference to cultural tradition. The main difference introduced by 'culture' seems to be that the men accused of an honour crime have typically killed what they viewed as a sexually wayward daughter or sister or cousin, while the standard pattern in 'non-cultural' cases is a man who kills his ex-lover or wife. In both kinds of case, however, there is a presumption that a woman's sexual behaviour can be enough to provoke a man to lose his self-control. Why is one attributed to the influences of culture and not the other? Would it not be more consistent to treat both cases as cultural – or neither?

My instincts incline me to the second option. In giving these examples, I do not want to make what I consider a more limited point about the bizarre or horrific practices of one culture being mirrored in the bizarre and horrific practices of another. In an influential contribution to debates on cultural location and specificity, Isabelle Gunning proposed a three pronged 'world-travelling' approach to the issue of female genital surgery: see yourself in your historical context; see yourself as the 'other' sees you; see the 'other' in her own context. She illustrated with a reversal of perception that made cosmetic surgery the 'bizarre and barbaric' practice.[13] Western feminists (herself included) express anger and revulsion at the practice of burning, cutting or removing female genitalia, but they might usefully consider how a practice like implanting polyurethane-covered silicone into one's breasts must appear to those not used to this practice; or how close to sacrilege the self-starving of anorexia and bulimia must appear to those who experience starvation and poverty as a daily part of their life. Gunning explains her use of the term genital surgeries rather than genital mutilation as an attempt to strike a neutral tone. The additional effect, of course, is to draw attention to a continuity between genital and cosmetic surgery.[14]

This placing of practices coded 'modern' and 'traditional', 'Western' and 'non-Western', along the same continuum has become increasingly common in feminist literature and debate. It is part of what happens in Narayan's juxtaposition of domestic violence in the USA with dowry-murders in India; it also features in Leti Volpp's juxtaposition of gender apartheid under the Taliban with the severe restrictions on women's reproductive rights favoured by Christian fundamentalism.[15] But if all we do is point out these similarities and continuities, there is a risk that challenging the dichotomy between modern and traditional becomes the only or main political activity. The continuity I want to stress is not that we all have our weird cultural practices. The continuity that strikes me is that so few of us are 'driven' by culture. As Volpp has suggested elsewhere, very often what is at stake is not 'culture' but 'bad behaviour'.[16] In working out who is most a threat to women's rights or their physical safety, it may be more telling to ask how close people were to their mothers or how generous they are to strangers than to find out about their religious beliefs and cultural traditions.

My own sense of the ordinariness of culture is informed by life in contemporary Europe, and, more narrowly, in cosmopolitan London where hybridity is almost the order of the day. But the relevant illustrations are not restricted to this context. Consider the successful, village-led, campaign against female genital cutting in Senegal, carried out under the auspices of Tostan (Wolof for 'breakthrough'), an educational NGO.[17] When women have been asked why they continue with what they know to be a dangerous and painful practice, they typically cite custom and tradition.[18] Genital cutting then seems a particularly clear illustration of the power of culture and the way it regulates people's lives. But the other way of reading this is to say that what sustains the practice is the knowledge that everyone else does it, the knowledge that your own daughters will become unmarriageable if your family is the only one opting out. In Gerry Mackie's analysis, this is essentially what was at stake in the Senegalese case.[19] In recognition of this, the women leading the Tostan initiative developed the device of the collective pledge: signing villagers up to a date when they would all simultaneously abandon the practice. With this guarantee that others would also relinquish the genital cutting of their daughters, it became much easier for everyone to follow suit, and one village collectively abandoned the practice in 1997, followed in the next year by representatives from another thirteen villages, and then, in a snowball effect, by another eighteen villages in a different area. In 1999, the government, which had been very supportive of the initiative, enacted legislation officially prohibiting genital cutting. What is striking about the story is how easy it proved to bring about the change. Loyalty to the practice turned out to be paper-thin. There was, it seems, no deep 'cultural' attachment, but more simply and practically the difficulty of breaking out unless others did so at the same time.

What stands out for me in this example is how similar people are.[20] The reasons village representatives gave for wanting to renounce the practice are much the ones that would be given by parents all over the world (wanting to ensure their girls' health, bodily integrity and human dignity); the reasons previously given for carrying on with the practice (not wanting to make their daughters unmarriageable) were equally lacking in mystery. This is not to say that there were no 'cultural' differences between the Senegalese villagers and villagers in rural France, or, indeed, between the Senegalese villagers and the Senegalese political elite; nor does it imply that we all make sense of our lives and our relationships in exactly the same way. It does suggest, however, that there was no special need to rely on cultural difference in making sense of either the persistence or the eventual ending of genital cutting. In popular usages of the term, there is a tendency to call on culture when faced with something we cannot otherwise understand. Or as Adam Kuper put it, when commenting on a burst of cultural theorizing in twentieth-century modernization theory: 'Culture was invoked when it became necessary to explain why people were clinging to irrational goals and self-destructive strategies . . . Culture was the fallback, to explain apparently irrational behavior'.[21] But there is no obvious irrationality in saying you want to stop doing something but do not feel you can do this until others do likewise. In the Senegalese case, there was no special need for culture as 'fallback', or for complex cultural readings to make sense of otherwise incomprehensible acts. The behaviour was readily explicable in cross-cultural, human, terms.

References to culture or religion can be similarly uninformative in the politics of what is variously termed the headscarf, hijab or veil. There is clearly a religious basis to hijab, though it is now commonly stressed that the Quran prescribes only modesty, and prescribes this for both women and men. The translation of this injunction into a requirement that women cover their heads, and, in some versions, virtually all their bodies, in the presence of men other than immediate family, is contested by many Muslims. Dress codes have, in fact, varied considerably across Muslim countries, and twentieth-century secularizing movements (most notably in Egypt and Turkey) often focused on the veiling of women as one of the practices that should be brought to an end. In the latter part of the last century, this trend went into reverse. In countries where Muslims are a majority – but also those where they are a minority – a new generation of young women adopted the hijab as part of their religious, sometimes also political, identity; and mothers who had fought vigorously for the freedom to bare their heads watched in consternation as their daughters resumed the practice. For some in the 'new veiling' movement, it may be appropriate to describe them as acquiescing in parental or paternal expectations that reflect long-established cultural practice; for others, it can be said they are acquiescing in a new kind of pressure exerted by men of their own age. But many are clearly making their own statement about their religious identity and beliefs, and pursuing their own understanding of what is required by a pious existence. As Saba Mahmood argues in her analysis of the women's piety movement in Egypt, we need to 'detach the notion of agency from the goals of progressive politics',[22] and recognize that submitting oneself to the requirements of one's religion can be a practice of agency rather than its denial.

I am arguing here for a dilution in the notion of culture: not so much that we should deny the existence or relevance of cultural difference, but that we should be far more wary about promoting the notion of people as products of their culture. This way of thinking about culture makes it too solid an entity, far more definitive of each individual's horizon than is likely to be the case. In doing so, it also encourages an unhelpful distinction between traditional and modern cultures. Much of the agonizing about whether 'we' (presumably enlightened secular liberals) should accommodate 'their' (presumably something different) cultural practices and traditions is premised on a distinction between modern and traditional, in which the moderns wear their culture so lightly that they can readily set it aside as the law or morality requires, while the traditionals are so much enclosed by the dictates and expectations of their culture that it would be cruel to expect them to behave in the same way. Yet it is not, I believe, helpful to justify cultural accommodations on the grounds that members of non-Western cultural groups have little choice but to obey the dictates of their culture. This treats the requirements of a culture as more transparent and unified than will be the case, a point already well made in many feminist analyses. It also treats the individuals who constitute that culture as more culturally determined than is likely to be the case. Culture is ordinary, not exotic; it is not a peculiarity of non-hegemonic, non-Western, groups, for each of us, whatever our cultural heritage, is shaped in some way by our culture. To be shaped, however, is not to be determined, and while individuals vary considerably in degrees of assertiveness and compliance, I do not think cultures divide into those that dictate and others that merely recommend. We are all shaped, but not many of us are driven.

Where does this leave me? There is a risk that it leaves me in the company of those who would prefer to end all practices of cultural accommodation. The problem to which multiculturalism proposes an answer is the disadvantaging of citizens who do not subscribe to the majority or hegemonic culture. This disadvantaging is said to happen through the imposition of seemingly universalistic codes of conduct, which then turn out to bear more heavily on minority groups. If I think the power of culture has been exaggerated, presumably I think people can more readily discard cultural tradition than has been claimed. If I think this, that threatens to do away with much of the basis on which democrats have argued for cultural accommodation. One of the risks, in other words, in the argument I have been pursuing is that I could end up so much minimizing the significance of culture that I leave myself with no basis for multicultural practice. My arguments may also prove deeply offensive to those who consider their culture very much as defining their sense of themselves and of what they should do. They could even reflect an ethnocentrism that sees everyone through the prism of my own experiences of 'culture', and concludes that for everyone – as for myself – culture cannot possibly loom that large.

What I would stress at this stage is the importance of not claiming to know in advance whether people are being disadvantaged by the unthinking imposition of a hegemonic cultural code. It takes closer examination to determine what cultural conventions, if any, have been written into supposedly culture-neutral norms; and closer examination to establish whether a particular matter is one on which people do act differently according to cultural expectations and norms. There is little hope of answering such questions without involving men and women, young and old, rich and poor, from the variety of cultural groups; and this then sets down at least one plank of multicultural policy, which is that policies need to be drawn up in ways that genuinely represent the full range of experience. There is little hope of arriving at the right answers if the people consulted are exclusively drawn from hegemonic cultural groups or have a vested interest in exaggerating the distinctiveness of non-hegemonic cultures. Religious leaders, for example, might have a vested interest in exaggerating the centrality of religion to the lives of their constituents, or men in exaggerating the centrality of norms of female submissiveness – just as a defendant in a murder trial might have a vested interest in exaggerating the extent to which he is 'driven' by culture. Multicultural societies need to ensure far more equitable participation of people from the full diversity of cultural groups in determining laws and codes and practices. As feminists have repeatedly argued, this also means paying careful attention to the balance of participation between women and men and young and old. The object of this is to ensure that cultural disadvantage is identified and remedied. But there should be no prior assumption that people's actions, attitudes and values are determined by their membership of a cultural group.

5

What's wrong with essentialism?

Work on feminism and multiculturalism increasingly summons up the spectre of cultural essentialism. Though I do not myself much like the term, this has been a persistent theme in my own work. Critique of cultural essentialism runs as a thread through many of the essays in a recent collection on *Sexual Justice / Cultural Justice*,[1] and figures in a recent 'mapping of the terrain' by Ayelet Shachar as the object of an entire school of 'post-colonial feminism'.[2] As its deployment in these works confirms, essentialism tends to be thought of as a bad thing. We do not, on the whole, say, 'that position is essentialist and that's why I like it'; or 'I have some sympathy with your argument, but find it insufficiently essentialist.' As Ian Hacking puts it, 'most people who use [essentialism] use it as a slur word, intending to put down the opposition'.[3]

Yet it is also commonly argued that we cannot avoid at least some kind of essentialism, that it is a politically necessary shorthand, or even, in some arguments, a psychologically inevitable feature of the way human beings think. Diana Fuss has argued that the essentialism/constructionism binary blocks innovative thinking, providing people with too easy a basis for unreflective dismissal.[4] Gayatri Spivak famously wrote of a strategic essentialism that could invoke a collective category – like the subaltern or women – while simultaneously criticizing the category as theoretically unviable.[5] Though she subsequently distanced herself from what she saw as misuses of the notion of strategic essentialism, the idea that we may have to 'take the risk of essence' in order to have any political purchase remains an important theme in feminist theory and politics.

From a different direction, it is sometimes said that while essentialist constructs are, in a sense, category mistakes – drawing the boundaries between peoples or things in the wrong place – there is not much point rubbishing them as analytically wrong, because, once in existence, they become part of our social reality. Thus, anthropologist Gerd Baumann simultaneously criticizes and accommodates an 'ethnic reductionism' that divided the population he was studying in Southall, London, into five religio-ethnic groups: Sikhs, Hindus, Muslims, African Caribbeans and whites. The categorization was, he argues, seriously misleading, privileging one kind of group identity over others that were more important, and obscuring the dynamic ways in which group boundaries are drawn and redrawn. For many of his older interviewees, it was a particular region of the Indian subcontinent (the Punjab, Gujarat, Bengal), or particular island of the Caribbean, that provided the key terms of self and other identification; for some of the younger ones, a new 'Asian' identity was being forged that cut across distinctions between Hindu, Muslim and Sikh. The static five-way categorization reduced or denied this complexity. It also misrepresented culture as 'an imprisoning cocoon or a determining force',[6] encouraging potentially racist stereotypes, and significantly underplaying the multiple and imaginative ways in which people negotiate their cultural identities. For all his criticism, however, Baumann does not consider it appropriate simply to dismiss 'folk reifications' as falsely essentialized constructs, for once they have entered into people's own self-definitions, they assume a life of their own.[7]

Some psychologists, meanwhile, have suggested that essentialist thinking might just be part of the human condition, meaning that part of the way human beings process complex information is to seek out a deeper property – what we might then term an essence – linking the things that look alike. If we conceptualize racist thinking, for example, as the presumption that visible differences of skin colour or physiognomy indicate something significant about other characteristics like intelligence or temperament, then maybe part of what sustains racist thinking is an innate tendency within the way we process information? Drawing on studies of pre-school children in Europe and the USA, Lawrence Hirschfeld notes that children as young as four understand racial types in terms of an underlying essence, attributing differences in skin colour to something heritable and fixed at birth, while seeing differences in body shape or occupation as more susceptible to change.[8] Though stressing that the use of race markers as a basis for dividing people up into different kinds may be specific to particular epochs and societies, he suggests that the tendency to create 'human kinds', and attribute to at least some of these a 'nonobvious commonality that all members of the kind share'[9] (an essence, in other words), is built into our conceptual system. He is not saying it is impossible to eradicate notions of race from our mental repertoires, but makes the plausible point that telling children race is unimportant (as in the advice that 'we are all the same inside') will not be the most effective strategy if it fails to accord with a deeply rooted tendency to think in terms of essentially differentiated groups. The particular features we employ to identify groups will be shaped by history; but the process of identifying a group by some presumed essence may not be so.

Even setting aside the still contested terrain of conceptual systems, it is clear that theoretical analysis depends on at least some process of abstraction. This typically involves separating out something deemed core from other things deemed peripheral, so appears almost by definition to involve claims about accident and essence. Sociologists from the days of Max Weber have been encouraged to hone their analytical tools through the construction of ideal types, while analytic philosophers characteristically develop their arguments by stripping away misleading 'contingencies' in order to identify essential points. If we take essentialism to mean the process of differentiating something deemed essential from other things regarded as contingent, this can appear as a relatively uncontroversial description of the process of thought.

Like most of those who use the term, I continue to think essentialism a bad thing, but what exactly is wrong with it? Is it a matter of degree, a question of context or something that must be avoided at all costs? In what follows, I identify and discuss four distinct meanings. The first is the attribution of certain characteristics to everyone subsumed within a particular category: the '(all) women are caring and empathetic', '(all) Africans have rhythm', '(all) Asians are community oriented' syndrome. The second is the attribution of those characteristics *to* the category, in ways that naturalize or reify what may be socially created or constructed. The third is the invocation of a collectivity as either the subject or object of political action ('the working class', 'women', 'Third World women'), in a move that seems to presume a homogenized and unified group. The fourth is the policing of this collective category, the treatment of its supposedly shared characteristics as the defining ones that cannot be questioned or modified without undermining an individual's claim to belong to that group.

The four are clearly not identical, so one might be engaged in essentialized thinking on one score while managing to avoid it on others. Indeed, one of the ironies of essentialism is that social critics challenging the structures of thought that sustain racism and sexism commonly attack the first two versions, but are often criticized in their turn for falling into the third or fourth. It is, in fact, in our political engagements that we are most likely to fall foul of one version of essentialism or another. By the beginning of the twenty-first century, it is hard to find reputable scholars who can be plausibly castigated for their deployment of essentialized categories: we have most of us been sufficiently sensitized to the dangers to avoid such talk. In our political activities, by contrast, or in policy advice that divides populations into distinct religio-ethnic communities or assesses forms of engagement with this or that 'community', those essential-isms often retain their force. Rogers Brubaker argues that it is 'central to the *practice* of politicized ethnicity' to cast ethnic groups, races or nations as protagonists, and make claims in their name, and his main concern is that academic analysts should not uncritically adopt these vernacular categories as their own.[10] In his view, it is a category mistake to criticize the *political* practice of essentializing or reifying an ethnic group, for 'reifying groups is precisely what ethnopolitical entrepreneurs are in the business of doing'.[11] I do not share his insou-ciance as regards the political practice. It is in our political activities and discourses that essentialism is most alive today. This is where it most needs to be challenged.

Essentialism I

The first problem with essentialism is the attribution of particular characteristics to everyone identified with a particular category, along the lines of '(all) women are caring and empathetic', '(all) Africans have rhythm', '(all) Asians are community oriented'. The 'all' in such claims is usually implicit rather than stated, and allowance is com-monly made for individual exceptions. It would, however, be a mistake to regard this as absolving the assertion from criticism: as the phrase about it being the exception that proves the rule suggests, acknowledging exceptions does nothing to weaken the impact of the general rule. When a category that applies to billions (like women) is being employed, even the most rigid of essentialists will anticipate exceptions. Investing such categories with explanatory force still remains an extraordinary leap.

That said, there will often enough be *some* basis for the attribution. It is unlikely that the choice of characteristics is entirely random; and there may well be some observed history that lends itself to the claim. But the correlation might be statistically insignificant, and, even where it is statistically strong, the attribution turns what is only probabilistically true into a much stronger claim. The problem here is one of over-generalization, stereotyping, and a resulting inability even to 'see' characteristics that do not fit your preconceptions. In practice, this leads to discrimination: 'I would never employ, marry, believe an X, because they are all unreliable.'

There is plenty of research suggesting that the typical correlations are indeed misleading and overstated. As regards gender differences, it is widely thought that girls have better communication skills than boys and that boys are better at maths, that women are more empathic than men and men more aggressive than women, that girls and women are better at routine tasks while boys and men are better at complex problem solving; and there is indeed some evidence to substantiate these common beliefs. Yet when Janet Shibley Hyde examined 124 meta-analyses of gender difference, she found the gender differences close to zero, or small, in 78 per cent of cases.[12] There *were* differences, but the leap from this to claims of the form '(all) women x' or '(all) men y' was clearly unfounded. The studies approximated the stereotypes in only a few areas: Hyde reports moderate to large differences in throwing velocity and distance (one thinks of Iris Marion Young's famous essay on 'Throwing Like a Girl'[13]); in attitudes towards casual sex (men liked this more than women); and in physical – though less so verbal – aggression. In some of the most interesting results, Hyde reports the enormous power of self-stereotyping according to dominant gender codes in 'creating' gender difference. In one such example, men and women were divided into two mixed groups and asked to complete the same maths test. The first group was told beforehand that the test was thought to contain a certain gender bias, the second that it was gender-neutral. The men did better than the women in the first group, but there were no significant gender differences in performance in the second. Hyde concludes her analysis with a warning about the social costs of overinflated claims of gender difference.

Similar points can be made with regard to inflated claims of cultural difference. As I argue throughout this book, exaggerated discourses of cultural difference are commonly employed to represent young women from ethnic minority backgrounds as peculiarly in need of state protection, and essentialized constructions of oppressive (ethnic minority) families and victimized (ethnic minority) young women then contribute to a climate in which governments find it acceptable to impose illiberal bans on activities involving minority ethnic groups. The decision of the French National Assembly to ban schoolchildren from wearing 'conspicuous' displays of religious or political allegiance in public schools (in intention and effect, banning the Muslim headscarf) is one obvious example, for at least part of the justification for this was the claim that headscarves were being imposed on Muslim schoolgirls by family and community pressure. The policies adopted across Europe of restricting the entry of fiancés or spouses from outside the European Union until the potential marriage partners are variously eighteen, twenty-one or twenty-four is another telling illustration. Setting aside, for the purposes of argument, suspicions about the main object being to reduce non-white migration, the rationale is that this protects young people from coercion into marriage, for it is mainly young people of non-European origin who are exposed to the dangers of forced marriage, and it is plausible to think they will be better able to withstand parental pressure when they are twenty-one or twenty-four than when they are sixteen. Different minimum ages for marriage to partners from inside or outside the EU are then justified by claims about the greater exposure to familial coercion and lesser ability to resist it for young people in minority ethnic groups. These claims reflect and reproduce damaging cultural stereotypes.

I do not contest the claim that individuals are being coerced – that some French schoolgirls adopt headscarves because of their fears of being harassed or denounced as impure, or that many young people are forced into unwanted marriages – but I take issue with the kind of racial profiling that generalizes from evidence that *some* young people marrying partners from outside the EU are unwilling participants to a presumption that *all* such marriages are bogus. I do not think it appropriate to impose blanket bans on an entire practice because of evidence that some of those engaged in it are being coerced. I object to the failure to recognize that young people from minority ethnic groups can be as clear in their own minds about the choices they are making as young people anywhere; and I believe that an essentialized discourse of minority cultures, as almost defined by their tendency to coerce and constrain, has combined with an essentialized discourse of the victimized young women from minority groups to legitimate these illiberal policies.

Yet, as Ian Hacking reminds us in his sceptical take on social constructionism, something might have an extra-theoretical function – might, for example, encourage racist or sexist ways of viewing people – and yet still be true. Unmasking a function does not in itself add up to refuting a claim.[14] It has, moreover, been a key tenet of feminist and critical race theory that there are costs to denying as well as to exaggerating difference. Arguing for gender equality on the grounds that there are *no* differences between women and men can mean an over-ready acceptance of dominant scales of value. Arguing for racial equality on the grounds that we are all the same under the skin can suggest that some skin colours are indeed problematic. Arguing for cultural equality on the grounds that people are all fundamentally the same can suggest there is therefore no cost to being expected to align your own cultural practices with those of the dominant group. An unreflective critique of essentialism may not sufficiently address these concerns.

Acknowledging difference is not necessarily essentialist. Even profiling is not all bad. Kasper Lippert-Rasmussen notes that we do not usually consider it outrageous if the police work on the assumption that the perpetrator of a violent crime is more likely to be male than female; and even those strongly opposed to racial profiling tend to think it a waste of police resources if they search for the perpetrator of a racist hate crime among the victim's own racial group.[15] As regards forced marriage, while I reject blanket bans, I do not consider it outrageous if police and social workers draw up lists of risk factors that help them identify the young people most likely to be at risk of coercion into marriage. Any such list is clearly open to stereotyping and misrepresentation, and it will often be the case that the harms associated with this – the potential demonization of particular minority groups, and the treatment of young people from these groups as particularly passive victims – outweigh any advantages. But if we want societies to take effective action against problems such as forced marriage, targeting information and resources where they will be most effective looks a sensible idea.

This suggests that what is wrong with this first kind of essentialism is to some extent a matter of degree. We can all agree that over-generalization, stereotyping and an inability even to perceive characteristics that do not fit our preconceptions are problems; but the very use of the term *over*-generalization may then be the important point.

It is hard to see how any structured analysis of social and political issues is possible without abstraction and the deployment of (then always potentially stereotypical) generalization. What else, after all, is induction? Uma Narayan argues that 'antiessentialism about gender and about culture does not entail a simple-minded opposition to all generalizations, but entails instead a commitment to examine both their empirical accuracy and their political utility or risk'.[16] This suggests a continuum rather than an embargo, at least on this first version.

Essentialism II

In the second version of essentialism, characteristics are attributed not to the individuals making up a particular category, but to the category itself. So, it is *because* you are a woman that you are more caring than a comparable man, not because you live in a society where girls and women are expected to be more caring, or a society where family policy encourages a division of labour between male breadwinners and female carers. This is probably what most people understand by essentialism: not merely a perception of groups as different (with the associated risks of over-generalization), but the attribution of these differences to some underlying and static 'essence'. This move naturalizes differences that may be historically variant and socially created. As regards gender or race, this typically involves a biological or genetic determinism. As regards nationality or culture, it typically involves a reification that produces the 'nation' or the 'culture' as an entity in itself. As Rogers Brubaker puts it, the latter commits the error of 'groupism': 'the tendency to take discrete, sharply differentiated, internally homogeneous and externally bounded groups as basic constituents of social life, chief protagonists of social conflict, and fundamental units of social analysis'.[17]

It is easy to see why this kind of essentialism is problematic, though, again, there are risks in overstating the case. We should surely criticize discourses that naturalize socially and historically constructed differences: that attribute, for example, women's lesser participation in the world of high politics to a genetic difference between the sexes. We should also, in my view, resist the more modest notion that social differences are 'grounded' in nature, because differences involve categories, and categories are the kind of thing that only human beings produce. I take this to be an important part of what Judith Butler argues in her critique of the sex/gender distinction.[18] Thinking of 'gender' as a socially variable construct built upon a pre-given biological 'sex' is not enough to save us from the charge of essentialism, for in accepting without question the naturalness of the founding male/female divide, we concede too much to the norms of heterosexuality, and to the practice of grouping people according to their reproductive organs. Why not group people according to height? Why not according to the length of their little finger? The reason, obviously enough, is that we live in societies that attach enormous significance to reproductive complementarity, and need therefore to know whether someone is biologically 'female' or 'male'. But that is already a social explanation: the choice of salient distinction is not simply given to us by nature. It is itself a social act.

The other point to stress is that the naturalizing of socially and historically generated difference is not restricted to those categories most open to biological or genetic determinism, but can also figure in relation to ones that are self-evidently social and historical. Nations, for example, come into existence at particular periods of history, so even those with the most ethnocultural conception of nation or nationality must know that these cannot be defined in biological or genetic terms. So where is the essentialism here? I would locate it in the reification, the construction of nation or culture as *entity*. When people talk of 'cultural practices', or seek to explain the strange behaviour of their neighbours by reference to something termed their culture, they conjure up a simplified and homogenized *thing*. As Tariq Modood puts it, 'rich, complex histories become simplified and collapsed into a teleological progress or unified ideological construct called French culture or European civilization or the Muslim way of life'.[19] It is one thing to talk of there being culturally specific ways of expressing joy or mourning the dead or ordering relations between women and men. It is quite another – and far more troubling – to say that 'culture x' organizes gender relations in one way and 'culture y' in another. The first way of talking abut cultural difference is always vulnerable to stereotypes, over-generalization and the rigidity that fails to perceive when similarities are greater than difference (open, that is, to the worries attached to Essentialism I), but can also be relatively uncontentious. The second way of thinking about cultural difference commits us to culture with a capital 'C', culture as the explanation of everything members of a cultural group do or say, culture as *either* culture x *or* culture y, culture as profound difference. It commits us to an essentialist version of culture.

Essentialism III

The critique of stereotypes has been a staple of the feminist and anti-racist diet for years, and Essentialisms I and II have come in for their fair share of attack. The irony, as many feminists and critical race theorists acknowledge, is that movements to combat the hierarchical structures that generate and sustain these stereotypes often invoke a collectivity that itself seems to presume a unified, perhaps essentialized, group. Feminism, for example, challenges absurdly overstated generalizations about women and men, attacks discriminations and exclusions on the grounds of gender and, in some versions, argues for a world beyond gender. Susan Moller Okin, for one, argues that 'a just future would be one without gender. In its social structures and practices, one's sex would have no more relevance than one's eye color or the length of one's toes.'[20] Yet any movement to achieve such a goal necessarily invokes women, may indeed make a virtue of women organizing autonomously *as women,* and often calls for gender-specific measures that treat women differently from men. This invocation of the very categories under attack is part of what Joan Scott calls the 'constitutive paradox' of feminism. As she puts it: 'Feminism was a protest against women's political exclusion: its goal was to eliminate "sexual difference" in politics, but it had to make its claims on behalf of "women" (who were discursively produced through "sexual difference"). To the extent that it acted for "women", feminism produced the "sexual difference" it sought to eliminate.'[21]

The 'women' brought into existence through this politics may, moreover, obscure many differences *between* women along axes such as class, sexuality, race, nationality or religion. Feminists have rigorously avoided inflated claims about the essential differences between women and men, but in the practice of feminist politics are likely to make all kinds of generalizations about 'women' or 'women's interests' or 'women's oppression'. These are not, to be sure, the kind of generalization that says women are good at routine tasks but bad at problem solving, but rather generalizations about women being discriminated against in employment or under-represented in politics or expected to assume primary responsibility for care. Yet these generalizations, too, can obscure significant differences of location and concern, and often mean that the experiences of (all) women are read off the specificities of one sub-group. When the sub-group standing in for the category as a whole is relatively privileged, this poses an especially acute problem: 'The feminist critique of gender essentialism does not merely charge that essentialist claims about "women" are overgeneralizations, but points out that these generalizations are hegemonic in that they represent the problems of privileged women (most often white, Western, middle-class, heterosexual women) as paradigmatic "women's issues".'[22]

Uma Narayan goes on to stress the irony: that in addressing the tendency towards gender essentialism, feminists sometimes replicated essentialized thinking at a new level. They accepted, that is, the injunction to attend more closely to differences among women and not presume that women throughout the world faced the same set of issues and concerns, but they sometimes did this through equally totalizing categories such as Western culture, non-Western culture or Third World women. It became important not to generalize from the experiences of 'Western women', because this was said to fail to recognize the specificities of 'Indian' or 'African' culture. Essentialized understandings of cultural or continental difference then replaced previously essentialized understandings of gender. I have said that there are costs to denying as well as to exaggerating difference, but too much anticipation of difference is also dangerous, and generalizations about how the people in particular cultural groups act, or what problems the women in those groups face, can be seriously misleading.

The worries about simplifying, homogenizing and stereotyping take us back to issues already discussed under Essentialism I. The more distinctive feature of Essentialism III is the way movements for political and social change conjure into existence (in their own minds at least) political actors like workers, women, peasants, 'the people', and the problems associated with this way of conceiving of social groups. When Gayatri Spivak made her much-repeated comments about the 'strategic use of positivist essentialism',[23] she was reflecting on the work of the Subaltern Studies group, and in particular their attempt to retrieve an 'insurgent' or 'rebel' or 'subaltern' consciousness from documentation written from the perspective of counter-insurgents. Claims about group consciousness look like essentializing claims, not just in the modest sense of generalizing from what may be very different individual experiences, but in the attribution of an essential personhood to a group. A loose categorization of multiple locations and perspectives then comes to figure almost as a person, capable of acting, willing, challenging and having a consciousness all of its own. Even if we repudiate the notion of individuals as having unified identities, the treatment of collectives as quasi-persons endows them with more unity than they can justifiably claim.

Can we, however, think politics without collectivities? Can we think collectivities without at least some kind of essentialism? In one illuminating discussion of this, Iris Marion Young utilizes Sartre's distinction between group and series to conceptualize gender as seriality. She recommends that we reserve the term group for self-consciously mutually acknowledging collectivities with a self-conscious purpose: reserve it, that is, for those historically specific and often short-lived moments when people do indeed combine together in a common project, and it becomes appropriate to describe them as part of a unified group. Groups come and go, however, emerging from and falling back into a less self-conscious and more passively unified 'series'. A series is defined by reference to material practices and structures: 'gender, like class, is a vast, multifaceted, layered, complex and overlapping set of structures and objects. *Women* are the individuals who are positioned as feminine by the activities surrounding those structures and objects.'[24] Much of the time, we may not realize we are part of this series, though it could become quickly apparent when we discover that we face shared constraints and limits. Even when we realize this, however, we may choose not to make membership of that particular series a defining part of our identity. Gender as seriality makes no strong claim about the unity of experience or unity of identity, and offers, in my view, a non-essentialist way of thinking of collectives. It also helps us understand the way a series can generate what is, genuinely, a group, and the way a group falls back into the relative passivity of the series, sometimes after succeeding in its political project, sometimes after failing.

Essentialism IV

The final way of thinking about essentialism is in some ways the most challenging, for this is an essentialism that comes into play precisely at the moment when the generalization fails and the stereotypes no longer work. This is essentialism at its most overtly normative: the treatment of certain characteristics as the defining ones for anyone in the category, as characteristics that cannot be questioned or modified without thereby undermining one's claim to belong to the group. So, you're not *really* a lesbian if you also sleep with men; you're not *really* working-class if you like opera; you're not *really* a Muslim if you tolerate non-believers.

The normative weight is sometimes imposed from the outside, by people so mired in their stereotypes that they find themselves compelled to re-categorize those who display aberrant behaviour. Unable to cope with the idea that activities, interests or qualities considered intrinsic to one category of person might be found in people belonging to another, they simply re-categorize the person. The more damaging cases are those where the normative weight is imposed from within the collectivity, so that people find themselves repudiated by what they had continued to consider their own community. At all of those moments when you are told that you are not 'really' Indian / working-class / a feminist / a Trotskyist / whatever, there is a kind of categorical coercion at work. You are being refused your own self-definition because you lack some attribute deemed an essential component of the category you have tried to claim.

Sadly, this kind of controlling, regulating and policing activity can characterize movements for social change as much as movements against it. Perhaps particularly at the moment when what Iris Young termed a series generates a self-consciously committed group, the group may devote much of its energies to policing its own boundaries and ensuring that members really are united by the same practices and concerns. It is a frequent comment on radical politics that groups can become more preoccupied with the finer points of contention between themselves and their closest political neighbours than with ostensibly larger areas of disagreement with mainstream political parties; and dissidents within are continually at risk of expulsion. It is also one of the perennial criticisms of identity politics that the identity in question can become a form of social control, to the point where one's choice of sexual partner or relationship to one's parents, or even one's holiday destination, can become the heated object of political debate. When this happens, the identity is being defined by reference to an essential defining characteristic, and those who do not fit are in trouble.

Of the various meanings discussed in this chapter, this last is the one where the essentialism seems most unambiguously wrong. Interestingly, it is also the version that comes least readily to the fore, perhaps because it is so patently grounded in non-naturalistic claims. When people say I cannot regard you as an x because your views or lifestyle break the defining codes of x-ness, the 'essence' is clearly a social not a natural attribution. If being Indian, for example, were a matter of nature, nothing you subsequently did or said could take it away. It is precisely because it is a social construct that we are able to describe people as no longer 'really' Indian, or no longer 'really' working-class, or no longer 'really' lesbian. This reinforces the point made in relation to Essentialism II: that it is a mistake to think of essentialism primarily in terms of nature or biology or genetics, for much of what we rightly criticize as essentialist is political or social or historical. Essentialism is a way of thinking not always so easily distinguished from more innocent forms of generalization. We cannot expect to find the key to that distinction in a distinction between the natural and the social.

6

When culture means gender: issues of cultural defence in the English courts

[handwritten margin notes: see Susan Moller Okin essay Is Multicultural Bad for Women?]

The notion of 'cultural defence' surfaced in American law journals in the mid-1980s, in the wake of a number of cases where defendants invoked the traditions of their culture to explain or mitigate their actions.[1] It subsequently figured as one of the areas of concern in the feminist literature on multiculturalism, where the reliance on 'cultural tradition' is widely regarded as legitimating crimes against women.[2] One much-discussed case is that of Dong-lu Chen, a Chinese immigrant to New York who battered his wife to death with a hammer some weeks after discovering she was having an affair.[3] At his trial in 1988, an expert witness testified that, in traditional Chinese culture, a woman's adultery would be conceived as an enormous stain on the man; that he would find it difficult to remarry if he divorced his wife for adultery; and that violence against wayward spouses was commonplace in China.[4] The judge accepted that Chen was 'driven to violence by traditional Chinese values about adultery and loss of manhood',[5] convicted him of second-degree manslaughter, and sentenced him to five years' probation. In another much-cited case, Kong Pheng Moua, originally from Laos, was charged with rape and kidnapping after abducting a young Hmong woman from her workplace at Fresno City College and forcing her to have sex with him.[6] At his trial in California in 1985, it was argued that he was acting in accordance with a traditional Hmong practice of marriage by capture, in which the man would establish his strength and virility by seizing the woman, and she would ritually protest his sexual advances in order to establish her virtue. Kong Moua was found guilty only of a lesser charge of false imprisonment, and was sentenced to 120 days in prison and a fine of $1,000. Of this, $900 was to be paid to his

[handwritten margin notes: people is cruel; People of the State of California US Kong Pheng Moua 1985]

victim in what experts regarded as the traditional form of 'reparation'.

In the American literature, the use of cultural defence has given rise to a polarized debate, with some suggesting it be formally established as a new kind of criminal defence (akin therefore to currently recognized defences like diminished responsibility or self-defence), and others that it be excluded from the courtroom. This latter position often draws on explicitly feminist arguments. In the aftermath of the Chen judgment, for example, the National Organization of Women argued that cultural defence should be inadmissible, because it so self-evidently reinforces patriarchal power.[7] In one influential critique, Doriane Lambelet Coleman argues that the use of cultural evidence weights the interests of defendants above those of victims, and is particularly damaging to women. While acknowledging the right of defendants to cite cultural factors as mitigating circumstances at the point of sentencing (itself a large concession), she argues that only culture-neutral evidence should be permitted in establishing the question of guilt. Thus 'a defendant who killed his wife upon discovering that she had strayed from the marital bed could interpose the traditional defense of provocation', but he 'would not get the benefit of arguing that in his particular culture, the shame and devastation is elevated'.[8] The courts need to demonstrate multicultural sensitivity, but should not allow for 'cultural defence'.

In this chapter, I focus on ways in which culture is currently invoked in criminal courts in England and Wales, exploring what problems, if any, these pose for women. I begin with an overview of the general issues (some more overtly gendered than others), then provide a brief background to multicultural practice and legislation in Britain before moving on to specific cases.

Why is cultural defence a problem?

What is 'cultural defence' and why is it perceived as a problem? One definition, by Paul Magnarella, is that a 'cultural defense maintains that persons socialized in a minority or foreign culture, who regularly conduct themselves in accordance with their own culture's norms, should not be held fully accountable for conduct that violates official law, if that conduct conforms to the prescriptions of their own culture'.[9] Jeroen Van Broeck argues that such definitions should be supplemented by a definition of cultural offence: 'an act by a member of a minority culture, which is considered an offence by the legal system of the dominant culture. That same act is nevertheless, within the cultural group of the offender, condoned, accepted as normal behaviour and approved or even endorsed and promoted in the given situation.'[10] The point of the addition is that Van Broeck believes there has to be a link between the offence itself and the defendant's cultural background before the courts should consider allowing a cultural defence. Just the general fact of being socialized into a different culture is not in his view enough: there has to be something about the cultural background that changes the meaning or moral status of the offence.

A classic illustration from the English courts is *R v. Adesanya*, in which a Nigerian mother was prosecuted for the ceremonial scarring of the cheeks of her nine- and fourteen-year-old sons.[11] In this case, the fact that the scarification would have been accepted as a normal part of Yoruba custom, and that the Nigerian community in Britain was probably not aware that the practice was contrary to English law, was felt to change the status of the offence. It undoubtedly helped that the children were said to be willing parties to the ceremony, that the scars were unlikely to leave permanent marks, and that the mother was deemed of excellent character. Mrs Adesanya was nonetheless convicted: in English criminal law, a minority custom cannot be a defence to a prosecution, unless this is explicitly allowed for in legislation. She was, however, given an absolute discharge.

The use of cultural defence raises four major issues. The most general is that it threatens to undermine legal universalism. This is not so much because it allows individual circumstances to be taken into account in sentencing (of itself, this is hardly contentious), but because, in its larger application, it threatens to elevate cultural membership above other considerations. Ignorance of the law, for example, is not normally accepted as a legitimate defence. Why then should an ignorance that derives from cultural difference, or a defendant's relatively recent migration, be acknowledged as a salient factor? And what of other groups whose perception of an offence may differ from that of the wider society, but in their case for political rather than cultural reasons? An unsophisticated Proudhonist who claims that property is theft is unlikely to cut much ice when he uses this to explain why, in his world, it is entirely legitimate to appropriate his landlord's property. Why then should a Rastafarian be able to argue that smoking *ganja* conforms to the prescriptions of his religion, and is not an offence within his culture? The English courts have never accepted this last argument,[12] but the general point remains. Is it appropriate to single out either cultural membership or religious beliefs as entitling people to differential treatment under the law, or does this veer too far in the direction of different laws for different communities?

Cultural defence can also lend itself to opportunistic defences. Claims about what is normal within a particular cultural group are notoriously tricky. Something may be claimed as a cultural practice when it has long been contested or abandoned by other members of the group; and individuals who have largely adopted the practices and conventions of the surrounding culture may suddenly 'rediscover' an allegiance to a different culture because it now serves their interests to do so. In the civil courts, there may be strong financial incentives to identify oneself with a different legal tradition when this offers more favourable inheritance or divorce settlements. Similar issues inevitably arise in criminal cases, where judges may have to struggle with the question of whether defendants really are, as they claim, shaped by the prescriptions of a minority culture, or are just using this to secure some legal advantage. It is not always easy to determine which cultural influences might be acting on an individual. In the absence of any transparent test, the use of cultural defence could leave itself open to considerable manipulation.

The third, and more specifically feminist, argument is that cultures operate to sustain male power: Susan Moller Okin tersely comments that 'most cultures have as one of their principal aims the control of women by men'.[13] If so, then allowing cultural tradition as a legitimate element in a criminal defence could be said to encourage and sustain patriarchal practices. The cases that have come up in the British courts include ones where men have been charged with sex with an under-age girl, and have represented this as more 'normal' within the context of their countries of origin;[14] or been charged with the murder of a family member, and have referred to their cultural background to explain the disgrace brought upon the family by the sexual behaviour of their victim.[15] Culture has been successfully invoked in the US courts as a defence against charges of rape and murder, though the fact that the same two cases figure so prominently in the literature suggests these are an exception rather than the rule. The cultural conventions referred to in such cases are often deeply patriarchal.

Cultural defence does not, however, simply equate with male interests: we cannot say that culture is only invoked to let men off the hook for their crimes against women. In the (also much-discussed) *Kimura* case, a Japanese-American woman tried to drown herself, and succeeded in drowning her two children, after learning of her husband's adultery.[16] At her murder trial in California in 1985, it was claimed that this constituted a traditional Japanese practice of parent–child suicide (*oyaka-shinju*); that a wife shamed by her husband's adultery might choose suicide as the more honourable course of action; and that she would think it cruel to leave her children to live on without her in conditions of disgrace. In this case, the cultural evidence was not used to suggest that the practice was excusable, but rather to establish Fumiko Kimura's mental instability at the time of the offence. She was convicted of voluntary manslaughter, sentenced to one year's imprisonment, five years' probation, and instructed to undergo counselling. This brought the penalty closer to what would have happened in Japan, where attempted parent–child suicide is regarded as a crime, but is usually punished with a rather lenient sentence.[17]

Weighing up the pressures on a deeply distressed woman against the risks of condoning the murder of a child is, of course, notoriously difficult, and there have been other US judgments where a self-evidently disturbed mother has been treated far more harshly. But however one assesses the *Kimura* case, it is clearly not an instance of the woman losing out from the use of cultural defence. The more nuanced point made by Okin is that, even where the woman could be said to benefit, the cultural message is still thoroughly gender-biased.[18] The Kimura judgment implicitly normalizes and legitimates the deep shame felt by a woman faced by her husband's adultery, rather than in any way challenging this presumption. Even if individual women may sometimes benefit from cultural considerations, women as a whole could be said to lose out.

The fourth concern over the use of cultural defence is that it lends itself to stereotypical representations of the non-Western 'other' – what Pascale Fournier describes as a 'vulgar use of culture'[19] – and that in these representations, both men and women may be diminished. In one Canadian case (*R v. Lucien*, 1998), two men in their early twenties, both originally from Haiti, were convicted of sexual assault on an eighteen-year-old girl. Though the penalty for gang-rape normally ranges between four and fourteen years, they were sentenced only to eighteen months' curfew and community service. Noting their lack of remorse (usually a factor that would bring a more severe penalty), the judge suggested that it arose 'from a particular cultural context with regard to relations with women', and described the defendants as 'two young roosters craving for sexual pleasure'.[20] In this case, the invocation of culture not only meant that a crime against a woman was treated with unusual leniency. It also conveyed what many saw as a racist slur on Haitian men. Complaints were filed against the judge with the Quebec Judicial Council, which accepted, however, that she was referring to certain groups of youths – rather than specifically black or Haitian – when she spoke of cultural context, and did not in the event reprimand her.[21]

On one level, this example reinforces arguments made by Okin and Coleman about culture being deployed to excuse men's crimes against women, but because it also draws attention to the dangers of racist or cultural essentialism, it generates a more complex position. The Okin/Coleman critique has been said to promote this very essentialism – to accept, that is, that non-Western cultures are indeed more sexist, more patriarchal, more tolerant of violence against women – and make this the basis for rejecting cultural claims.[22] But what if these representations of the cultural 'Other' are themselves a part of the problem? Commenting on cases in the USA involving under-age sex or under-age marriage, Leti Volpp notes that culture is invoked in a highly selective way, so that virtually identical misdemeanours by white North Americans and non-white immigrants get attributed to 'culture' only when the defendants come from a racialized minority group: 'Behavior that causes discomfort – that we consider "bad" – is conceptualized only as culturally canonical for cultures assumed to lag behind the United States.'[23] This can clearly lend itself to 'vulgar' representations of culture, which could then justify the ill-treatment of women. Almost equally damaging, however, is the way it represents individuals from these 'lagging' cultural groups. Individuals from the dominant cultural group might be led astray or make mistakes, but are usually deemed as in some way responsible for their actions. No one suggests that 'their culture made them do it'; indeed their culture has become such a taken-for-granted background that it has been rendered virtually invisible. Individuals from minority groups, by contrast, are more commonly conceptualized as defined by and definitive of their culture, so that even the most aberrant can become 'typical' products of their cultural norms. In his judgment on the *Chen* case, Judge Pincus described Chen as 'the product of his culture':[24] the individual is read off the culture, and the culture off the individual in turn.

Though it arrives at it by a different route, it might be said that this analysis of cultural essentialism leads to much the same conclusion as the Okin/Coleman critique: that cultural defence is a highly dubious development, and ought to be stopped in its tracks. This is not, however, the conclusion reached by Leti Volpp, who cautions against 'an all-or-nothing approach that either precludes all cultural evidence, or admits it without challenge'.[25] Cultural evidence must, she argues, be interrogated for stereotypes, preferably by enabling competing narratives to be heard. But simply disallowing cultural evidence would encourage the false belief that the law has no culture, thereby leaving 'American identity, and specifically the identity of United States law, a neutral and unquestioned backdrop'.[26] When references to cultural difference are disallowed, this has the effect of confirming the (supposedly non-cultural) majority norm.

This is one of the key issues arising in the assessment of cultural evidence and cultural defence. It seems entirely plausible that existing legal practice will be imbued with the cultural norms of dominant groups. If so, then refusing to acknowledge cultural diversity puts members of minority communities at an unfair disadvantage. This is the danger highlighted by the UK Judicial Studies Board, which provides guidance to judges on matters of equality. In its *Equal Treatment Bench Book*, it stresses that 'recognising and curbing our prejudices is essential to prevent erroneous assumptions being made about the credibility of those with backgrounds different from our own', and offers as examples that 'looking down and lowering one's voice can be a sign of respect, but not every African-Caribbean or Chinese young male will conform to this stereotype'.[27] If cultural evidence is understood as explicating the different norms of behaviour that may operate in different groups, then it hardly seems at odds with legal universalism. It can be regarded, if anything, as a way of ensuring that these principles are met.

This perhaps enables us to resolve the first of the problems outlined above, but the others remain. Defendants could clearly employ culture in opportunistic ways, for, when faced with the prospects of a criminal conviction, one might well exaggerate the centrality of certain cultural practices in order to establish a legal defence. In relation to women, an uncritical use of culture could have two particularly damaging effects. First, it could encourage the courts to excuse, or at least mitigate, crimes against women, because it might lead them to accept such crimes as 'normal' within a different cultural context or different cultural codes. Secondly, it could diminish women (and men) from minority cultural groups by mis-representing their cultures, and mis-representing the individuals as less than autonomous beings.

Cultural practice in England and Wales

The practices associated with multiculturalism in Britain fall broadly into the category of extensions and exemptions. Some seek to extend to other cultural groups 'privileges' previously enjoyed only by members of the majority or dominant culture. Obvious examples are scheduling exams so as to avoid key festivals of a number of religions, not just the main Christian festivals; or extending the principle of state support for denominational schools (confined, until recently, to Anglican, Catholic and Jewish schools) to include schools for Muslims, Hindus and Seventh Day Adventists. Extensions are sometimes contested on the grounds of practicability – that there are just too many groups to take into account. Sometimes, more simply, the objection is that they *do* challenge the privileged status of the dominant culture. In most ways, however, extensions look the least controversial face of multicultural policy. The object is to redress a previous bias – sometimes deliberate, sometimes just unthinking – and ensure more equitable treatment. Because, however, they give added legitimacy to religious and cultural groupings, they can also work to strengthen the power of religious and cultural leaders over their members. For feminists in particular, they therefore continue to give cause for concern.

The more obviously controversial initiatives seek exemptions for members of particular cultural groups from requirements that are legally binding on other citizens, the usual justification being that conformity requires a much greater sacrifice of cultural values for some groups than for others. Examples include the exemption of turban-wearing Sikhs from the requirement to wear safety helmets on building sites or when riding a motorbike, or of Jewish and Muslim slaughterhouses from legislation governing the slaughter of animals. Those most firmly wedded to universal principles of justice may object that conformity to the law always requires more sacrifice from some people than others. Thus, libertarians may also have very strong objections to the law on crash helmets; or to cite a rather unhelpful analogy from Brian Barry, those strongly attracted to rape will be more severely disadvantaged by the legal prohibition on it than those who never felt the temptation.[28] What Barry terms the 'rule-and-exemption approach' is on the face of it more troubling to notions of citizen equality than the idea of extending to other groups privileges previously enjoyed only by one. It has, however, presented less of an issue for feminism, because the standard areas of exemption have so little to do with male power.

The relevant legislation in England and Wales mainly deals with matters of food and dress.[29] The Slaughter of Poultry Act (1967) and the Slaughterhouses Act (1974) allow Jewish and Muslim abattoirs to continue to slaughter poultry and animals according to traditional religious methods, basically exempting them from the requirement to pre-stun animals prior to slaughter. The Motor-Cycle Crash Helmets (Religious Exemption) Act (1976) exempts turbaned Sikhs from the requirement to wear protective helmets when riding a motorbike; the Employment Act (1989) similarly exempts them from the requirement to wear safety helmets when working on construction sites. The 1988 Criminal Justice Act prohibits people from carrying knives and other dangerous weapons in public, but specifically exempts knives that are carried for religious reasons. Though there is a gender subtext running through many of these examples – it is Sikh men, for instance, who wear turbans, not Sikh women – it would be hard to describe these exemptions as promoting gender inequality or conceding too much to patriarchal power. They do, of course, give a public validity to claims about cultural identity that might in later circumstances be employed to more damaging effect; but the immediate implications for gender relations are relatively innocuous.

In some of the areas that have been of more direct feminist concern, legislation has prohibited rather than exempted. Up until 1985, the position on female genital mutilation remained unclear. There was no legislation formally covering this and no cases establishing judicial precedent, but a number of reports suggested that operations were being carried out in the country. The Prohibition of Female Circumcision Act (1985) banned such operations except where they can be shown to be necessary for a person's physical or mental health, and explicitly excluded the belief that genital mutilation is a necessary 'matter of custom or ritual' as an illegitimate basis for exemption. The later Female Genital Mutilation Act (2003) did little more than change the name, and make it possible, in principle, to prosecute parents who took their daughters abroad for such operations.[30]

Under-age marriages, if legally contracted under a different jurisdiction, were condoned for a period, and the culturally relativist judgment in *Alhaji Mohamed* v. *Knott* might certainly raise some eyebrows today. In this case, a 13-year-old girl who had contracted a marriage with a 26-year-old man in Nigeria was committed to local authority care in England after a doctor alerted the police to her probable age. The care order was subsequently revoked by the Court of Appeal, which felt that what would be repugnant 'to an English girl and our Western way of life' would be 'entirely natural' for a Nigerian girl: 'They develop sooner, and there is nothing abhorrent in their way of life for a girl of thirteen to marry a man of twenty five.'[31] The judgment has been cited as a good example of cultural tolerance,[32] though, to my mind, it only appears so when set against the Eurocentrism of the Juvenile Court, which had deemed the continuation of the couple's association as 'repugnant to any decent-minded English man or woman'. Whatever one's view on this, under-age marriage is now illegal in Britain. In the mid-1980s, cases involving a 12-year-old Iranian bride and a 13-year-old Omani bride (both living with their student husbands) provoked a tightening of immigration regulations, and entry clearance is no longer granted to spouses if either party is under sixteen on the date of arrival.[33] Since those already in the country cannot legally contract an under-age marriage, there are no longer any circumstances in which such marriages would be condoned. As with female genital mutilation, this does not mean there are no de facto marriages involving girls under 16 years of age – but, legally at least, this is no longer an open issue.

The position on polygamy is complex, and again has been affected by changes to immigration rules. English law prohibits individuals who are already lawfully married from contracting a second marriage within England and Wales, and declares void any polygamous marriage (even a 'potentially polygamous' marriage[34]) contracted outside the country if either party is at the time domiciled in England and Wales. Since the 1988 Immigration Act[35] also prevents second and subsequent wives of polygamous men from joining their husbands in the UK for settlement purposes, there is virtually no scope for recently contracted polygamous relationships. The limited recognition given to polygamous marriages (both to the valid ones and to those declared void) has been mostly to women's advantage, and it would be a pretty harsh imposition of universal monogamy not to allow these concessions. The children of such marriages are recognized as legitimate, and spouses are not prosecuted for bigamy. Divorcees and widows of potentially polygamous marriages are entitled to some forms of matrimonial relief and protection;[36] even when the marriage is declared void, the courts may still make orders for financial provision or the division of property; and the NHS pension scheme allows for a splitting of the widow's pension between two widows of a polygamous marriage.[37] Some feminists might regard this limited recognition as going too far in its acceptance of patriarchal marriage. Some pluralists argue that polygamous marriages should be accorded the same legal recognition as monogamous ones.[38] But the current balance would seem to work largely to women's advantage.

One point arising from this brief review is that most of the issues that might fall into Van Broeck's category of 'cultural offence' – an act by a member of a minority culture, which is considered an offence by the legal system of the dominant culture, but is condoned, accepted as normal, or approved of by the cultural group of the offender – have simply been taken out of the picture. Some such practices, like female genital cutting, have been banned. Others have been regulated through a combination of legislation, immigration rules and judicial precedent, to the point where there is little scope for legal dispute. It might, of course, be argued that these initiatives are themselves inappropriate: that public policy has been overly assimilationist on issues like genital cutting and under-age marriage, and that a more thoroughgoing multiculturalism is required. My own view is that claims forwarded on behalf of cultural integrity are particularly questionable when they relate to the treatment of minors, who have, by definition, little authority within their cultural group and suffer a double disempowerment by virtue of both sex and age. Leti Volpp's requirement for competing narratives of culture to be heard simply cannot be met when the key participant is only a few years old. And while one might reasonably query whether the 16-year-old who is assumed to know her own mind about the choice of marriage partner was so devoid of agency a few days earlier, when she was only 15, the risks of subordination to someone else's version of what is appropriate to one's culture must surely increase in inverse proportion to age. Where a minor is concerned, the claim that a practice is condoned, accepted as normal or approved by a cultural group is self-evidently open to abuse.

Where something akin to cultural defence arises in the English courts, it has been largely in respect of offences that would also be regarded as such within the defendant's culture, but where cultural factors might be said to mitigate the seriousness of the offence, for example by increasing the nature of the provocation or diminishing the responsibility of the defendant. The gender issues here replicate wider points made about the gendering of criminal responsibility.[39] Provocation, for example, is currently one of three pleas available to defendants for reducing a murder charge to one of voluntary manslaughter – the other two being diminished responsibility and suicide pacts. But because it relies on what has been viewed as a masculine model of 'a sudden and temporary loss of self-control', it has been less available to women subjected to months of physical or sexual abuse, who may act against their aggressor some time after his last assault. Aileen McColgan notes that this bias has to some extent been corrected in recent Court of Appeal judgments, but '(h)owever much the defence is tweaked and refined, the provocation plea is premised upon an angry loss of self-control . . . It is not designed to serve those who act in panic or fear, such as frequently appears to be the case when battered women kill their abusers.'[40] Meanwhile, the plea of self-defence – which, if successful, will lead to total acquittal – is more readily available to a man who matches his attacker in physical strength, and employs only what the courts will recognize as 'justifiable force'.[41] The limited applicability of either provocation or self-defence to women defendants makes them more reliant on a plea of diminished responsibility. So, where men can argue that their action was 'reasonable' in the circumstances (that the provocation was such as would lead a reasonable man to lose his self-control, or that the force employed was reasonably proportional to the attack), women must more often present themselves as less than rational agents. This suggests important parallels between cases in which culture is explicitly invoked, and ones where it is not perceived as an issue.

Representations of culture

Two early cases of cultural defence involved prosecutions for under-age sex: *R v. Bailey*, which involved the prosecution of a 25-year-old man from the Caribbean for intercourse with two girls aged 12 and 14; and *R v. Byfield*, where a 32-year-old, also from the Caribbean, was prosecuted for sex with a girl aged 14.[42] The girls were described as either 'precocious' or 'mature'. While this is itself a worrying move, implying that the children were somehow responsible for the course of events, there was no suggestion of non-consensual sex in either of these cases. Culture was invoked at the appeal stage as a relevant consideration in explaining why the men might be unaware that their actions were either unusual or unlawful. Bailey's nine-month prison sentence was reduced to a £50 fine, while Byfield was discharged after serving three and a half months of his eighteen-month sentence.

Culture intervened here in relation to penalty rather than guilt; and one gets a strong sense from these early cases (as also from *R v. Adesanyo*) that the judges felt they were dealing with a moment of transition from one set of cultural norms to another. In this context, it was felt important that the convictions should reaffirm the requirements of English law, but not appropriate that the individuals concerned should bear the full weight of the legal penalty. Bailey was said not to have known that his conduct was unlawful, and to be so shocked by his conviction that he was unlikely to repeat the offence. Byfield was warned that, whatever the social customs in the West Indies, he must in future comply with English law. The judgments sent a message to recent immigrants as to how they should conduct themselves, but the individuals who served as the occasion for the message were not dealt with too harshly. At this point, in other words, the courts could regard themselves as dealing with a one-off moment of accommodation: individuals in transition would be treated with some leniency, but, pretty soon, all citizens would have adjusted to 'how we do things around here'.

In later cases, the relationship between cultural background and knowledge of the law has been less prominent, and there is more of a sense that cultural pluralism may be a permanent rather than temporary phenomenon. Two kinds of cases have emerged that are of particular relevance for my argument: first, those where cultural context has been seen as significant in interpreting the actions of female defendants; second, those where 'culture' is invoked to mitigate severe acts of violence against women. The first category has been problematic because of the differential treatment accorded to women, depending on how closely they conform to images of female subservience; the second, more starkly, because it risks excusing the murder of women. The number of cases is too small to permit firm generalization, but it does appear that two of the problems identified above – the stereotyping of the non-Western 'Other', and the 'cultural' mitigation of male crimes against women – have arisen in English legal practice.

R v. *Bibi* has been described as '[o]ne of the best illustrations of how ethnic customs and values may affect length of a prison sentence'.[43] This is a case where a woman benefited from cultural considerations, and had her sentence cut as a result. Bashir Begum Bibi, a 47-year-old widow living with her brother-in-law Abdul Ali, had been sentenced along with Ali for her role in importing cannabis from Kenya. The cannabis was delivered to the house they shared, and Mrs Bibi had unpacked the contents. She was initially sentenced to three years' imprisonment and her brother-in-law to three and a half. Reviewing this similarity in sentence, the Court of Appeal noted that the social inquiry report on Bibi had described her as totally dependent on her brother-in-law for support, and socially isolated by her poor English. It suggested, moreover, that she was so thoroughly socialized into subservience that it was hard to consider her as an autonomous actor:

> it is apparent that she is well socialised into the Muslim traditions and as such has a role subservient to any male figures around her . . . Because she has assumed the traditional role of her culture any involvement in these offences is likely to be the result of being told what to do and

the learned need to comply ... In the light of that history, it would not be safe to credit her with the same independence of mind and action as most women today enjoy.[44]

The Court of Appeal reduced her sentence to six months.

The suggestion that Bashir Begum Bibi could not be credited with 'the same independence of mind and action as most women today enjoy' seems to go considerably beyond her level of complicity in the drugs offence towards a general denial of her status as an autonomous agent. While the decision itself strikes me as appropriate and compassionate, it still gives cause for concern that it drew on stereotyped notions of 'the Muslim traditions' and 'the traditional role of her culture'. It also gives cause for concern that this kind of defence differentiates so sharply between those who conform to prevailing images of female subservience and those who in some way deviate from this norm.

When Kiranjit Ahluwalia, for example, was tried for the murder of her physically abusive husband, the judge's directions to the jury tended to minimize the cultural considerations. He noted that her marriage had been an arranged one, but this 'may have been the custom'; he observed that her mother-in-law had advised Mrs Ahluwalia to separate from her husband if she did not like him, and commented that 'if it was really as bad as all that, it may have been the best thing to do'.[45] There is little acknowledgement here of the difficulties many Asian women have spoken of in exiting from an arranged marriage into a community that holds women responsible for the family honour. In one particularly revealing comment, the judge advised the jury that 'the only characteristics of the defendant about which you know specifically that might be relevant are that she is an Asian woman, married, incidentally to an Asian man, the deceased living in this country. You may think she is an educated woman, she has a university degree. If you find these characteristics relevant to your considerations, of course you will bear that in mind.' The only meaning I can give to this is that the jury might think she was more trapped in her marriage and less responsible for her actions because she was an Asian woman, but might also see this as cancelled out by the fact that she had a university degree.

Ahluwalia's murder conviction was overturned at subsequent appeal, largely because these directions had ignored medical evidence available at the time – though not used in the original trial – that she was suffering from a major depressive disorder. At this point, the judge laid more stress on her vulnerability, describing her as physically 'slight', as having suffered many years of abuse from the onset of her marriage, and trying to hold her marriage together because of her 'sense of duty as a wife'.[46] In this second judgment, Kiranjit Ahluwalia was represented in terms that more closely echoed the descriptions of Bashir Begum Bibi, appearing now as a passive victim of events.[47] What is striking, nonetheless, is the message implied in that original direction: that, were Kiranjit Alhuwalia the 'typical' victim of an abusive arranged marriage, the jury might be more inclined to see her as someone driven to desperate measures; but, since she was an educated woman, they probably shouldn't give this much weight. This suggests that 'culture' becomes available to female defendants only when they conform to prevailing images of the sub-servient non-Western wife. Culture then works to sustain certain stereotypes of the non-Western 'Other'.

The prevalence of such stereotypes has been one of the issues in the campaign to free Zoora Shah, released from prison in 2005 after serving nearly fourteen years for the murder of Mohammed Azam. At her initial trial in 1992, the prosecution had presented her as voluntarily involved in sexual relationships with at least two married men; seeking to secure from the first of these, Azam, the title deeds of the house she lived in (bought in his name but paid for with her money); conspiring with a second lover to forge Azam's name to a transfer of ownership; paying a hit-man to kill Azam; and, when this came to nothing, poisoning him with arsenic so as to stop the civil proceedings he had taken out against her. Zoora Shah gave no evidence in court, but denied the four charges against her.

When her case went to the Court of Appeal in 1998, the judgment revolved around three issues.[48] First, how was the court to weigh new evidence from medical practitioners (including a consultant psychiatrist with experience of trans-cultural psychiatry), suggesting Shah was suffering from a severe mental disorder at the time of the murder, against medical evidence from 1992 suggesting she was anxious and depressed but not suffering from a severe depressive illness? Second, was it permissible to introduce a plea of diminished responsibility when this was not used at the initial trial, or did this go against the 'one trial' principle? Third, was the new evidence Zoora Shah now provided on the course of events to be regarded as 'capable of belief'? Through many months of meetings with Pragna Patel of Southall Black Sisters, Zoora Shah had told of being abandoned by an abusive husband, befriended by Azam, a heroin dealer, who had beaten and raped her and encouraged his associates to visit her for sex, and finally putting a powder in his food when he began to show a sexual interest in her 12-year-old daughter. A statement based on these interviews was put before the Court of Appeal. If the story was true, however, why hadn't she told it before? Why had she confided in no one through all those years of physical and sexual abuse?

In their assessment of this last question, the judges accepted 'up to a point' 'the importance of honour in the society from which the defendant springs', and the particular difficulties a woman like Zoora Shah might have faced in making public a history of sexual abuse. But only up to a point,

> because the appellant, as it seems to us, is an unusual woman. Her way of life had been such that there might not have been much left of her honour to salvage, and she was certainly capable of striking out on her own when she thought it advisable to do so, even if it might be thought to bring shame on her or to expose her to risk of retaliation.

Honour, by implication, attaches to the sexually chaste or the dutiful wife, while those exhibiting any capacity for action cannot hope to be believed when they say they were constrained by shame or fear. The fact that one of her daughters described her as a 'strong-willed woman' seems also to have told against her. You cannot, it seems, be both strong-willed and abused by others; you have to be either the helpless victim wronged by others, or someone capable of wrong-doing herself. In the case of Zoora Shah, cultural context is raised but not seriously addressed, and one is left feeling that culture will only be recognized as relevant when women conform to a particular stereotype. A woman portrayed as entirely under the control of male family members may draw on beliefs about non-Western cultures to make a claim for diminished responsibility, but if she is sullied by past sexual encounters or over-qualified by virtue of a degree, she no longer fits the prevailing image. There is little room here for the complexity of most individuals' lives.

When we turn to the second category of cases – those where religious or cultural beliefs are cited as partial defences against charges of murder – the courts have proved largely resistant to arguments that invoke a cultural defence. The common pattern in honour killings is the murder by family members of a young woman said to have sinned against religious or cultural prescription by her actual or presumed sexual behaviour. The total number of such cases is unclear: a retrospective investigation by the London Metropolitan Police identified 109 killings that might have involved issues of honour; this compares with around 110 women killed annually in the UK by current or ex-boyfriends, partners or spouses. The number where any kind of cultural defence is offered has been tiny.

In one much-publicized case, the victim was 19-year-old Rukhsana Naz, who had been married at 16 to her second cousin, had two children from this marriage, but lived separately from her husband who remained in Pakistan. When she later became pregnant by a boyfriend she had known since her schooldays, she was strangled by her brother Shazad, with the assistance, it was charged, of her mother and younger brother.[49] The defence of Shakeela and Iftikhar Naz centred on whether they did indeed participate in the killing (in the event, the younger brother was acquitted of involvement in the murder). However, a plea of provocation was submitted on behalf of Shazad Naz, who was said to have been provoked by the revelation of his sister's pregnancy into a sudden and temporary loss of self-control. His 'idealistic' religious beliefs were invoked to explain the intensity of the shame he felt on learning of his sister's condition, and the jury was asked to consider whether Rukhsana's conduct was such as to cause 'a reasonable and sober person' of her brother's 'age, religion and sex' to act as he did. They decided, unanimously, that it wasn't, and both Shazad and Shakeela Naz were convicted of murder.

Cultural considerations were introduced in this case, but not accepted as justifying the plea of provocation, and the judge commented in sentencing that 'this was a particularly horrific offence, involving as it did the murder of a young pregnant woman, who was already the mother of two children, at the hands of her own family'. Cultural issues also surfaced briefly in the appeal case of the mother, when her counsel referred to the section in the *Equal Treatment Bench Book* that warns against ethnocentric assumptions, and the danger that a jury might erroneously deploy 'their own assumptions to evaluate the behaviour of those whose cultural conventions are different from their own'.[50] But the key issue in Shakeela Naz' appeal was whether the jury had been properly directed on evidence relating to her own involvement. Since her defence had been that she was attempting to restrain not assist her son, she could not also invoke questions of family honour in her defence. Her conviction was upheld on appeal.

In 2002, Faqir Mohammed killed Shaida, his 24-year-old daughter, with a knife, after discovering her (fully clothed) boyfriend in her bedroom.[51] Here, too, the defendant submitted a plea of provocation. Here, too, the 'provocation' revolved around religious beliefs. In considering the plea, jury members were instructed to take into account Mohammed's depression (he had been treated with anti-

depressants after the death of his wife) and his 'strongly held religious and cultural beliefs'. The judge accepted, in other words, that
Mohammed could legitimately cite his belief that a daughter should
not have a boyfriend without his consent, and his strong conviction
that sex outside marriage was a grave sin, as possible causes of his
loss of self-control. But '[a] man may not rely on his own violent
disposition, by way of excuse', and jury members had to weigh the
depression and religious beliefs against evidence from six of his children that he was a man with a history of violence towards his children
and wife, who had a greater tendency to violence than was 'reasonably normal'. In this case, the jury rapidly came to the conclusion
that Mohammed was guilty of murder. He was sentenced to life
imprisonment.

The exception to this pattern is the case of Shabir Hussain, who
was convicted in 1995 of murdering his sister-in-law, Tasleem Begum,
by driving into her while she waited on a pavement for her lover,
and reversing the car over her body. At the initial trial, Hussain
denied his involvement, so there was no question of him submitting
a plea of provocation based on either culture or religion. He was
convicted of the murder and sentenced to life imprisonment. He successfully appealed against this conviction on the grounds of false
identification,[52] and it was at his retrial in 1998 that he introduced
a plea of guilty to manslaughter by reason of provocation. The provocation was hardly one that would have stood ground were it not for
cultural factors: all that Tasleem Begum had done was to default on
a marriage arranged for her in Pakistan when she was sixteen, refuse
to sign the documents that would have enabled her husband to get
a UK entry visa, and later embark on an affair with a married man.
In his judgment, however, the judge acknowledged that her illicit
affair 'would be deeply offensive to someone with your background
and your religious beliefs', and sentenced Hussain 'on the basis that
something blew up in your head that caused you a complete and
sudden loss of self-control'.[53] (This resonates with the Chen case,
where the judge commented that '[t]he culture was never an excuse,
but it is something that made him crack more easily'.)[54] Hussain's
original life sentence was cut to six and a half years.

The contrasting treatment of Shabir Hussain and of Zoora Shah
– both of whom lied at the original trial and both of whom introduced new defences the second time round – gave rise to extensive
media commentary, and certainly gives ground for thinking that
cultural defence is loaded against women. The key point in the
Hussain case was not so much the sentencing. Six and a half years is

not far out of line with the normal tariff for manslaughter of seven to eight years; the judge explicitly stated that he saw the case as falling towards the top end of the sentencing bracket, and that it was 'very difficult for anyone hearing the account of what happened to understand what you did and why you did it'; and the minor mitigation was partly because the defendant had eventually pleaded guilty. The key point is that the prosecution accepted the new plea of guilty to manslaughter by reason of provocation, possibly (though this is speculation) because of anxieties about securing conviction when the initial murder verdict had been overturned on appeal. Once the provocation plea was accepted, the sentence was more or less predictable.

With this troubling exception, the English courts have not been particularly receptive to provocation pleas based on intensely held religious beliefs about pre-marital and adulterous sex, or cultural understandings of honour and shame. Yet one is left wondering what might have been the outcome for Faqir Mohammed if he had had no previous history of violence towards his children; or for Shazad Naz if the horror of his actions had not been so much intensified by the fact that his mother was also involved. The fact that a defendant can legitimately cite the shame brought on his family by a sister's or daughter's transgressive behaviour remains disturbing, and, since this evidence could potentially reduce a murder charge to the lesser one of manslaughter, it promises to affect not only the question of penalty but also the question of guilt.

One might imagine a parallel case in which a member of a white racist organization claimed he had been put under unbearable pressure by seeing his sister with a black lover, and, in a moment of madness, took her life. In this hypothetical case, the defendant might also believe that his sister's behaviour was an insult to the family honour and degraded the family name, but it is hard to imagine any court today accepting this as provocation. One obvious reason for the difference is that there is legislation against racism, but no law (and rightly so) against thinking pre-marital sex a sin. But the contrast potentially returns us to one of the questions posed in the opening discussion: should intensely held religious convictions be treated differently from intensely held political convictions? Should 'culture' be elevated above other concerns?

The other way to view these cases, however, is in the context of the much larger category of 'non-cultural' murder cases where men invoke the provocation of an unfaithful or nagging wife to secure the lesser conviction of manslaughter: cases that themselves involve shared cultural assumptions about 'normal' wifely behaviour, but do not present these in explicitly cultural terms. The murder cases discussed above do not, on the whole, suggest a pattern of differential treatment for defendants from minority cultures, and they compare with a much larger category of cases where male violence had been rendered explicable without any reference to cultural tradition. Indeed, the main difference introduced by 'culture' is that these men killed what they viewed as sexually wayward sisters or daughters. The more typical pattern in other cases has been a man who kills his ex-lover or wife. Culture has been invoked, not so much to explain a heightened reaction to what is perceived as transgressive sexual behaviour, but to extend the class of legitimately incensed males beyond the immediate confines of lovers or spouses. The common thread, however, through both 'cultural' and 'non-cultural' cases, is the presumption that a woman's sexual behaviour can be enough to provoke a man to lose his self-control.

In these, as in all the cases discussed here, 'culture' operates within a terrain already defined by mainstream gender assumptions: the idea that sex with an under-age girl is more excusable when she is 'mature' or 'precocious'; that women are not really responsible for actions undertaken under the direction of male family members; or that men explode into rage when they discover their women involved in illicit affairs. References to the defendant's cultural background can ratchet up the characteristic in question. Thus, Mrs Bibi was credited with little independence of mind and action, and was said to be very different from the average woman in this; Shabir Hussain killed in circumstances that might cause other men to shout and swear. But Bibi's subservience only made sense because it resonated with what has been perceived as a general female characteristic, while Hussain's violence towards his sister-in-law fell within a recognizable spectrum of male behaviour. By contrast, neither Zoora Shah nor (in her first trial) Kiranjit Ahluwalia fitted prevailing images of the vulnerable woman: the first because she was 'strong-willed' and had lived too long in a criminal sub-culture; the second because she was over-qualified. In some ways, it seems a misrepresentation to treat any of these as 'cultural' cases. What we see, rather, are pretty standard conventions of gender difference, given an added twist or intensity through what are perceived as cultural codes.

Commenting on parallel cases in the USA, Daina Chiu makes the important suggestion that American courts only recognize 'cultural' factors when these resonate with mainstream American norms. Dong-lu Chen, for example, got off lightly for killing an adulterous wife,[55] but the anger of a wronged husband is hardly unique to

Chinese culture, and American courts could readily recognize what he did as a standard 'heat of passion' act. When Kong Moua expressed his surprise that the woman who resisted his sexual advances really meant it,[56] his incomprehension resonated with widely shared beliefs about women saying 'no' when they really mean 'yes'. The public sympathy for Fumiko Kimura depended less on her Japanese background and more on a wide-spread American perception that to live with the knowledge that you have killed your children is the worst punishment any woman can face. As Chiu tellingly notes, when Quang Ngoc Bui killed his three children and tried, but failed, to kill himself in desperation about his wife's affair (on the face of it, a very similar set of events), his cross-cultural evidence cut no ice with the court. Unlike Kimura, he was convicted of murder, and his death sentence was later upheld on appeal. An otherwise 'good' mother who kills her children in pitiable circumstances can be viewed as an object of compassion; a man who kills his children is likely to be seen as pitiless and cruel.[57]

The suggestion here is that cultural evidence only 'works' when it enables judges and juries to fit the defendant's actions into a pattern already familiar through mainstream culture: that, in the end, it is the sameness not the difference that matters. Invocations of 'culture' are themselves pretty clearly gendered. They convey for women a particular stereotype of passivity, and for men a meaningful context for violent actions, and are then likely to figure for men in diminishing the severity of their actions, and for women in diminishing who they are. But this gendering of cultural expectations resonates with a wider gendering of criminal responsibility that can leave women defendants with no option but to establish their mental impairment, whilst allowing men the additional recourse to provocation or self-defence. The content of the defences also draws on established norms of gendered behaviour: in Moua's case, the belief that many women make a play of resisting men's sexual advances; in Chen's, that violence is a normal male reaction when faced with an unfaithful wife. It is when 'culture' echoes gender norms in the wider society, or gendered practices in the law as a whole, that it is most likely to be recognized as an excuse.

Conclusions

There are two main conclusions to this. First, while none of the cases identified from the English courts is as disturbing to notions of natural justice as *People v. Moua* or *People v. Chen*, there are clearly some problems with the way cultural evidence has been employed. In the Hussain case, the court was over-receptive to a defence drawing on codes of family honour, and, while not 'excusing' the killing of a sexually active young woman – Hussain was sentenced to six and a half years – the judge accepted in mitigation that her behaviour had put the defendant under unusual pressure. In the treatment of female defendants, meanwhile, 'culture' seems to be allowed or disallowed depending on conformity to cultural stereotypes, leading to both an inconsistency of treatment between different cases and a perpetuation of those stereotypes.

This first conclusion might suggest that courts should now abandon their attempts to recognize cultural diversity while avoiding cultural excuse, and adopt the more straightforward 'culture-neutral' route advocated by Doriane Lambelet Coleman. This is at odds, however, with my second conclusion, which is that the difficulties that arise in the use of cultural evidence are themselves part of a wider pattern. It is largely when mainstream culture itself promotes a gendered understanding of agency and responsibility – as when it perceives men as understandably incensed by the sexual waywardness of their women, or women as less responsible for their actions because of the influence of men – that references to cultural context have proved effective. If this is so, then it is not the use of cultural evidence per se that is peculiarly gendered. It is not that this has unusually dire consequences for women, and ought on that basis to be curtailed. Such a position would suggest that gender inequities enter only at the moment when a minority cultural context is invoked, that the default position already secures the equal treatment of women, and that this is only threatened when 'culture' is allowed to intrude. Pleasing as it might be to think so, this hardly fits with the large literature in feminist legal theory,[58] and is certainly at odds with (government as well as academic) concern about the treatment of rape and male violence against women.

Cultural arguments work when they enable judges and juries to fit what might otherwise be deemed extreme or incomprehensible behaviour into familiar patterns. Chiu puts it thus: 'The jury will process evidence about another seemingly foreign and different culture only to the extent that the jury can relate to it and understand it. Thus, where the jury finds common ground with the defendant, its deliberation and verdict become an exercise in recognizing cultural sameness, not difference.'[59] She sees this as a criticism – that what looks like an accommodation of difference is in truth a re-imposition of sameness – but I am inclined to think this is the best one can hope for in the context of a court. The implication, however, is that, when the outcome of the process is judgments that favour men over women or defendants over victims, the reasons will lie in the dominant rather than minority culture. It is not the introduction of cultural evidence per se that generates problems in the equitable treatment of women, for such evidence only has the desired effect when it resonates with mainstream conventions.

The argument here links with more general questions about whether gender can be theorized in isolation from culture, and the dangers (much debated in the feminist literature) of setting up these two as separate and distinct. One problem is that women in minority cultures are thereby rendered invisible, or rather are swallowed up in what are said to be their cultural traditions, which are then presented as more unified and uncontested than is ever the case. The problem on the other side is that gender equality comes to be attached to those who are deemed to have no 'culture' – becomes attached, in other words, to the dominant culture, where the relationship between the sexes is presumed to be more emancipated and less patriarchal than is the case within minority cultural groups. The further problem that emerges from this chapter is that, when gender and culture are theorized as distinct, any gender inequities that arise out of cases invoking cultural considerations will be misread as effects of 'cultural defence'. This in turn will lead to the view that there has been too much accommodation of minority cultures, and that this is why women are disadvantaged.

I have suggested, against this, that cultural arguments only work when they resonate with mainstream views. Some of these will be mainstream understandings of non-Western culture, as exemplified in the perception of Asian women as passive and subservient to men. Others will be mainstream conventions about masculine behaviour, as in the readiness to accept that men are provoked beyond reason by a woman's sexual betrayal. In either case, it seems that the problem lies as much with the gendered conventions of the dominant culture as with the introduction of a cultural defence. It cannot be resolved by the elimination of 'culture' (which in this context is always understood as 'minority culture') from the courts, for this would unfairly discriminate between defendants from majority and minority cultures, permitting only the first to give full details of their individual circumstances and background. It would, moreover, promote the misleading notion that patriarchal norms characterize only minority cultures, and thereby encourage a false complacency about majority gender norms. 'Culture' operates on a terrain already defined by mainstream gender assumptions, and the gender inequities that have been associated with the use of cultural defence need to be understood within this context. The uses and abuses of cultural defence highlight issues that have much wider provenance, and direct us to a more thoroughgoing challenge to patriarchal norms wherever these appear.

7

Free to decide for oneself

The freedom to decide for oneself has been both aspiration and worry for feminists. The worry stems mostly from the emphasis on deciding 'for oneself', which seems to associate freedom with the ability to separate oneself from others. This has been felt to reflect an egotistical and over-individuated conception of the self, and a large and varied literature on maternal feminism, relational feminism and care feminism has developed alternative formulations.[1] Others defend the focus on the individual as a crucial part of the feminist project.[2] Whatever position one adopts on these debates, it is clear that some version of autonomy is going to remain a defining element in feminism. Through the centuries, women have been required to submit to husbands chosen by fathers, to religious injunctions regarding the appropriate forms of sexuality and motherhood, to paternalistic legislation claiming to 'protect' them from their own frailties, or just to the expectation that a good woman will sacrifice her own needs or ambitions to the needs of those she loves. Generations of feminists have argued that women need a stronger sense of self in order to challenge the many constraints on their lives.

They have also explored, in subtle and complex ways, the difficulties in achieving this. Writing in the 1940s, and through the prism of existentialist philosophy, Simone de Beauvoir was particularly concerned by the 'bad faith' that comes with women's lack of freedom. In a passage that still rings disturbingly true, she describes the way women may compound their own impotence by refusing to accept responsibility for their lives.

A free individual blames only himself for his failures, he assumes responsibility for them; but everything happens to woman through the agency of others, and therefore these others are responsible for her woes. Her mad despair spurns all remedies; it does not help to propose solutions to a woman bent on complaining: she finds none acceptable. She insists on living in her situation precisely as she does – that is, in a state of impotent rage.[3]

From de Beauvoir's perspective, no one ever really loses the freedom of action and choice. But the constraints that mould women into 'women' can make it virtually impossible for them to exercise this freedom in the world, leading to narcissism, masochism or that state of impotent complaint.

Writing in the 1990s, and with a particular focus on India, Martha Nussbaum was more struck by the failure to rage against the world, by the way women can become so habituated to an unequal division of income and resources that they end up thinking themselves as of lesser worth than men.[4] As the literature on adaptive preferences has stressed, people have an extraordinary capacity to ignore those things they feel they cannot change, or to undervalue those opportunities they know to be closed to them.[5] So while some (like de Beauvoir's women) will indeed rail against the injuries done to them, others quietly adjust their sights to what they perceive as possible. For Nussbaum, the exercise of freedom therefore depends on the development of certain capabilities. It is only when public policy promotes bodily health, bodily integrity and the capacity to reflect critically on our lives (to list only three of her central human capabilities) that the freedom to decide for oneself becomes meaningful.

These are two examples from a wide range of perspectives, but already they indicate some of the problems in distinguishing a 'free' from an 'unfree' decision. The woman described by de Beauvoir feels very strongly that she is *not* free. She blames everyone but herself for her impotence; she refuses to accept responsibility for the choices she has made; it is always her husband or society or fate that is to blame. De Beauvoir is not unsympathetic to this predicament – she is not saying the woman should simply pull herself together and take responsibility for her own life – but she does see the inability to recognize yourself as a free person as one of the markers of women's oppression. For Nussbaum, by contrast, too many women think they are free when in fact they are not; they take for granted a particular ordering of society or family, and fail to see that the order is unjust.

This is putting it too crudely, but it is as if de Beauvoir wishes women could get beyond the complaining to acknowledge themselves as free beings, and Nussbaum that they could get beyond the resignation to acknowledge the extent to which they are unfree.

An alternative route – not much followed by feminists – is to define a free decision as one that was not physically forced.[6] It would then be evident enough, from the bound hands or pistol to the head, when people were *not* acting freely; and in the absence of overt force, it would be safe to assume that people did what they wanted to do. The fact that some people enjoy a wider range of options than others – perhaps because they are wealthier or have accumulated more qualifications, perhaps because they are male, or white, or young – would have no bearing on whether their decisions were freely made. Nor would it be considered relevant that some people are more subject than others to the pressures of family, religion or community. Anyone who lives in the world (that is, everyone) is subject to pressures and constraints, but precisely because this is true of everyone, it makes no sense to try to disentangle the things we 'really' want from those we were coerced to do. If we give in to the enticements of a successful advertising campaign, does this mean we were 'forced' to smoke? If we succumb to the attractions of a higher income, does this mean we were 'forced' to work in the private sector? Or to take the example I want to address in this chapter, if young people give in to parental blackmail and the threat of ostracism by their community, does this mean they were 'forced' into marriage?

I suspect that most readers will baulk at an understanding of freedom that equates it with 'not physically restrained', and will want to introduce some distinction between decisions actively embraced and those to which people resign themselves because of a lack of alternatives or pressure to conform. But the conundrums of freedom have been debated for centuries, and not come much closer to settlement, and even if we take as our starting point that the freedom to decide for oneself implies something more substantial than not being legally prevented or not being physically restrained, many of the problems remain. My concerns in this chapter arise from some considerations regarding gender equality in a context of cultural diversity; more specifically, they arise from the contrast between voluntary and coerced that is implied in the distinction between arranged and forced marriage. As indicated in the next section, there are a number of difficulties in the way this distinction is currently being mobilized.

I argue that Carole Pateman's enormously innovative discussion of freedom and subordination in *The Sexual Contract* offers a possible route for resolving these.

To anticipate, Pateman notes that assessments of the validity of contracts tend to revolve around the conditions under which people enter an agreement. Many have argued that what looks like a free agreement is in reality often coerced, because the person entering it had no real alternatives. Standard examples in the literature include the worker who 'agrees' to work for below-subsistence wages, because all the employers in the area have formed a cartel and none will offer higher wages; or the woman who 'decides' to become a prostitute, because all the more respectable forms of employment are closed to her once employers learn about her illegitimate child. Though no one technically forced these individuals, it seems inappropriate to say they freely agreed; and it is widely felt that their lack of alternatives undermines the validity of their contracts. The key innovation in *The Sexual Contract* is that it focuses our attention on a second aspect. Even when nothing is awry in the conditions under which people made their decision, the agreement might still be problematic if it involves submission to another person's power. As Pateman put it:

> A great deal of attention has been paid to the conditions under which contracts are entered into and to the question of exploitation once a contract is made. Proponents of contract doctrine claim that contracts in everyday life match up well enough to the model of the original contract in which equal parties freely agree to the terms; actual contracts thus provide examples of individual freedom. Their critics, whether socialists concerned with the employment contract, or feminists concerned with the marriage contract or prostitution contract, have countered this claim by pointing to the often grossly unequal positions of the relevant parties and to the economic and other constraints facing worker, wives and women in general. *But concentration on coerced entry into contracts, important though this is, can obscure an important question: does contract immediately become attractive to feminists or socialists if entry is truly voluntary, without coercion?*[7]

According to Pateman, it is not just the 'bad' contracts we must be wary of, for we need to recognize that contract itself can be inimical to freedom. I argue that this deeper critique of contract helps clarify what is at issue in the distinction between forced and arranged marriage.

The problem: arranged and forced marriage

The right to determine one's own choice of marriage partner is increasingly recognized in schedules of human rights. Yet many young people are forced into marriage against their will, not (as in the staple of nineteenth-century European literature) because they can see no other means of subsistence, but because their families insist on them accepting a particular marriage partner, chosen for reasons of property, religion, family status or caste. Familial pressure to marry within one's own ethnic or religious group operates across all cultures, and the statistics on the proportion of marriages that cross class or ethnic boundaries (very few) make for depressing reading. The chances of being *forced* into an unwanted marriage are, however, especially high in societies that practise arranged marriage, for it is when it has become the norm for parents to take the decision about the choice of marriage partner on behalf of their children that the temptation to insist is most likely to arise. Paradoxically, the chances of being forced into marriage against one's will may also increase as the practice of arranged marriage wanes, for parents may become more strident about their right to dictate the choice of spouse precisely because the young people are becoming more insistent on their own right to choose. There is some evidence that this may be the case among second and third generations settled in Europe. Families often spring into action on the marriage front when they discover that their young people have formed what they regard as inappropriate relationships – perhaps with someone of a different religion or ethnicity, perhaps just someone felt to be of bad character – and the parents then start searching for what they hope will be a more 'traditional', less Westernized spouse, very often from their own countries or regions of origin.[8] In such cases, the insistence of the parents may grow in direct proportion to the reluctance of their children, and what was initially conceived as an arranged marriage becomes forced. It is not easy to estimate the scale of this problem, for, as with rape and domestic violence, the reported figures largely depend on whether people think public authorities are acting effectively to address it. The material discussed here derives from initiatives against forced marriage in the UK, where the figure commonly cited is 1,000 young people forced into marriage each year. This is widely regarded as an under-estimate, and a recent study suggests the correct figure is closer to 4,000.[9]

Documented cases include ones where parents or other family members have kidnapped an under-age girl, taken her out of the country and held her in captivity until she 'agrees' to the marriage. Though a determined minimalist might quibble that no one was man-handling the girl when she went through the ceremony, these cases come as close as one can imagine to the bound hands or pistol to the head, and would be recognized by most as instances of forced mar-riage. Others are less clear-cut, and part of the difficulty in developing an effective public strategy against forced marriage is that it is not always evident whether a marriage is forced or arranged. Coerced entry into a marriage contract can take many different forms, and would not always be described as such even by those most affected. The language used by a group of young South Asian women in London to describe their marriages makes it pretty clear that most of them felt they had no power to refuse. '[Y]ou just have to go along with it', says one; 'if you didn't there would be just hell to pay from your parents and all your relatives'.[10] But none of these interviewees described her marriage as 'forced'. They may have succumbed to emotional blackmail, they may have gone along with their parents' preferences because they felt they had no other choice, but they did in the end 'agree'. Given the almost inevitable grey areas between coercion and persuasion, how are we to distinguish between mar-riages arranged by parents on behalf of their children, but voluntarily accepted by the children, and those arranged by parents *against* their children's wishes, that should more rightly be regarded as forced?

In principle, the distinction is clear, and revolves around consent: 'In the tradition of arranged marriages, the families of both spouses take a leading role in arranging the marriage, but the choice whether to solemnise the arrangement remains with the spouses and can be exercised at any time. The spouses have the right to choose – to say no – at any time. In forced marriage, there is no choice.'[11] But, of course, people say no, and later agree, or say yes because they cannot face the consequences of refusal: are we to say that all such marriages are therefore voluntary? The notion that marriage should be based on consent is common to all religions, and it is hard to imagine any cleric conducting a marriage ceremony with one or other of the potential spouses held under restraint or refusing to go through the forms of agreement. So if the marriage happens, then, at one level, the spouses must have agreed. The question is what kind of pressure was exerted on people to make them agree, and at what point this might be said to vitiate the consent.

The largest survey currently available in Britain was carried out in the mid-1990s as part of an investigation into *Ethnic Minorities in Britain*. Those surveyed were of South Asian origin (this being the largest group in Britain practising arranged marriage) and comprised Hindus, Muslims and Sikhs. The investigation was undertaken, however, before there was much public awareness of the phenomenon of forced marriage, and the questions were framed in ways that make it difficult to get at a distinction between forced and arranged. Several levels of parental involvement were distinguished: 'Parents made the decision'; 'I had a say but parents' decision'; 'Parents had a say but my decision'; 'I talked to my parents but my decision'; 'I made decision on my own'; and a category for those who 'can't say'.[12] Parental involvement remained high for all groups, with only 20 per cent of younger Indian respondents and 8 per cent of younger Bangladeshis and Pakistanis saying they made the decision on their own. For a majority of the older respondents, the parents were not just involved but actually made the decision; this had become a minority experience for most of those under thirty-five, the exception at that time being Muslim women, two-thirds of whom still reported that their parents made the decision. Parental *involvement* seems too large a category even to qualify a marriage as arranged, for it potentially catches in its net any family where young people talk over current boyfriends or girlfriends with their parents, and seek their opinions on who might make a good spouse. Parental *decision*, on the other hand, must include a mixture of arranged and forced. If the parents made the decision, this could mean that the young people had no strong opinion on the matter (unlikely but not impossible); that they initially disagreed but were eventually persuaded to their parents' point of view; or that they continued to disagree but were overruled. For those falling into the last two categories, there has to be a question mark over the degree of consent.

This is, in fact, increasingly recognized in the courts, where there has been a growing awareness of the complexities surrounding consent. Up until the early 1980s, petitioners to the English, Welsh and Scottish courts seeking the annulment of what they claimed to be a forced marriage had to establish that they had been frightened into agreement by a 'genuine and reasonably held fear' of danger to 'life, limb or liberty'. The courts operated, in other words, with a robustly self-sufficient notion of responsibility, and petitioners had to establish some version of the pistol to their heads. The principle had been established in 1971 in the influential case of *Szechter* v. *Szechter*, which involved a marriage of convenience, entered into in order to extricate the woman, who was in poor health, from a Polish prison where she was being held for anti-state activities. Though the petition was successful, the judge was careful to stress that it was 'insufficient to invalidate an otherwise good marriage that a party has entered into it in order to escape from a *disagreeable* situation' (my italics). There had to be – as in this case there was – a more substantial threat to liberty or life. When subsequently applied to cases of forced marriage, this ruling had predictably harsh effects, for the kind of pressure parents exert on children in order to get them to accept a favoured marriage partner is more commonly emotional than physical.

From the early 1980s onwards, the courts have increasingly acknowledged this, and have eased up on their initially robust view of coercion to recognize the diffuse ways in which vulnerable young people can be forced into marriage against their will. In *Hirani* v. *Hirani* (1983), the court took into account the applicant's age (she was nineteen at the time of the marriage) and her financial dependence on her parents, as well as the evidence that her (Hindu) parents had arranged the marriage in order to prevent her association with a young Muslim man. Concluding that the crucial question was not whether she was in fear of her life or liberty, but whether her mind had been overborne, the court granted a decree of nullity. In *Mahmood* v. *Mahmood* (1993), the court took the young woman's age and 'cultural background' into account in assessing whether her parents' threat to cut off financial support and send her to live in Pakistan could be seen as overriding her will. In *Mahmud* v. *Mahmud* (1994), it granted a decree of nullity to a thirty-year-old man who had been made to believe that his persistent refusal to marry had brought about the death of his father. In *Sohrab* v. *Khan* (2002), the video of the wedding ceremony, showing the bride's unhappiness, was used as evidence that she had not freely given her consent. All these judgments recognize that there is more to free consent than simply the absence of physical force. On the interpretation of duress being employed in these decisions, many of the marriages currently described as arranged would more properly be regarded as forced.

I applaud the legal developments, but they still leave tricky questions about the nature of free decision and the meaning of consent. In part, they recognize that decisions can come with almost unbearably high costs attached: the cost to a vulnerable young woman of losing her family's financial and emotional support; or the cost to a loving son of carrying the blame for his father's death. In such cases, the costs of continuing to reject the proposed marriage were indeed high. But what made them so overwhelming as to invalidate the apparent consent? We would not, presumably, wish to invalidate *every* decision arrived at under emotional or financial pressure, so what is it that marks out these ones as different? Chandran Kukathas has argued that the fact that certain decisions come with high costs attached is irrelevant, for while '[c]ost may have a large bearing on the decision taken . . . it has no bearing on the individual's freedom to take it'.[13] 'No bearing' is surely too cavalier, but it is true that there is a cost attached to every decision (you have to give up something, if only time, in order to do something else), and that the size of the cost does not seem to be the deciding factor. His own example is the Chief Executive who is offered a billion dollars not to leave his position to become a university professor. This makes the decision to leave extremely costly, but we would hardly conclude that it makes him less free to go. Or consider the more commonplace example of the highly paid company executive who is deciding whether to give up her career in order to look after her child full-time. Measured in terms of loss of income and loss of social status, it will be more 'costly' for her to do this than for her sister, who works for low wages in the local supermarket, to make the same decision. All other things being equal, the two women could find themselves living a similarly precarious existence; since one gave up so much more than the other to be with her child, we can say that the costs attached to her decision are considerably higher. But this does not seem enough of a reason to say she had *no* choice, nor is it so obviously a reason to say she had *less* of a choice. Indeed, when the higher cost reflects a position of privilege (the company executive has been earning more than her sales assistant sister for years), it seems odd to represent it as reducing her freedom of choice.

This is one concern. The other is that arguments that depend on vulnerability to cultural norms and expectations can perpetuate stereotypes of minority cultural groups. In the cases noted above, the legal judgment was informed by a perception of the typical South Asian family as more close-knit than is the norm across Western Europe, and as correspondingly harder for its members to challenge. This is most explicit in *Mahmood* v. *Mahmood*, where the young woman's 'cultural background' was cited as explaining why she might have been particularly vulnerable to her parents' threats. She was, by implication, less able than a girl from a different background to assert herself against her parents, and more likely to succumb to their pressure. This may or may not be sociologically plausible, but it says, in effect, that 'culture' makes people less capable of autonomous action, and less responsible for what they do. As noted in chapter 6, when this kind of argument is attempted on behalf of defendants in criminal cases, feminists will mostly reject it. 'My culture made me do it' is not regarded as an acceptable defence for a man who has killed an unfaithful wife or a father who has killed what he viewed as a sexually wayward daughter; and with a few disturbing exceptions, the courts in Europe have not been sympathetic to this type of defence. So is there a potential inconsistency here? If 'cultural background' can be used to explain away a woman's seeming consent to a marriage, can it not also be used to explain away a man's violent reaction to his wife's infidelity? If vulnerability to cultural expectations and family pressure can cast doubt on the significance of a consent to marry, why not extend the same compassion to defendants in so-called 'honour crime' cases?

We can, perhaps, extricate ourselves from the seeming inconsistency by insisting that criminal cases be judged by more stringent criteria than those involving the dissolution of a marriage, but, even if we do so, we are left with the worrying implication that women from a minority ethnocultural group are less capable than others of giving their consent. One of the points repeatedly highlighted by Carole Pateman in her analysis of patriarchy is the tendency to treat a woman's consent as inherently unstable. The most notorious examples come from rape cases, where defendants have successfully argued that they understood the woman's 'no' as really a 'yes'. We have not yet seen the last of this, but the once wide-spread perception of women as less than autonomous beings is no longer so pronounced. It lingers on, however, in the treatment of women from minority or non-Western cultures. As I have already noted, when 'cultural background' is offered in the American or European context as a reason for thinking that seeming consent was in reality enforced submission, the move is almost entirely reserved for women from minority cultural groups. One might go further and say it is almost entirely reserved for women from a racialized minority. Compare what happens when someone socialized within a Christian, Jewish or secular culture takes a marriage partner. We may find ourselves puzzled by their choice. We may, on occasion, observe that they ended a previous relationship with a partner disliked by their parents and settled for someone more in tune with the class, religious or racial preferences of their family (this is not an unusual occurrence). But we still, on the whole, regard it as 'their' choice, and do not describe the decision to marry as submission to an all-powerful family. The marital choices of women from minority or non-hegemonic cultures are, by contrast, more likely to be regarded as inauthentic. It is when

Muslim or Hindu or Sikh women take a marriage partner favoured by their families that it becomes more common to question whether they really gave their consent.

The presumption that young people from minority cultural groups are less able to act autonomously has already had some disturbing consequences in public policy. As I have noted elsewhere, European governments have looked to immigration control as one way of containing the phenomenon of forced marriage. They have focused, that is, on cases involving spouses from abroad, devoting much less attention to cases of coercion that involve spouses already in the country, and have introduced restrictions on the age of marriage partners coming into the EU, and the age of those sponsoring their entry. The declared object is to protect vulnerable young people from coercion into unwanted marriages, the argument being that they will be better able to withstand family pressure when they are older. The effect, however, is to infantilize ethnic-minority women. In the Danish legislation, a woman planning to marry an overseas partner has to reach the ripe age of twenty-four before she will be regarded as acting on her own initiative. Under the less draconian UK regulations, she has to be twenty-one before she can be trusted to know her own mind. Without in any way understating the pressures brought to bear on young people to get them to submit to an unwanted marriage, I find that blanket tendency to discount decisions made by younger people in minority cultures deeply worrying. Public policy does not, on the whole, ban an entire practice because of evidence that some individuals are being coerced into it. This becomes the standard response only when it is presumed that certain groups of people do not (or cannot) know their own mind.

Sawitri Saharso has addressed this tendency to deny women's autonomy in her analysis of multicultural policy in the Netherlands.[14] She gives as one illustration a public discussion that took place in the late 1990s over the supposed use of sex-selective abortion, and whether the Dutch legislation should be tightened to prevent abortion on the grounds of sex. The presumption was that certain minority groups in the Netherlands had a cultural preference for boys, were using ultrasound scanning to identify female foetuses and then arranging for their abortion. (Saharso notes that there is no evidence that this was a wide-spread practice.) In one revealing contribution, a newspaper journalist suggested that a Muslim woman requesting the abortion of a female foetus could not be regarded as expressing her own desire or choice, but only as reflecting a culturally imposed requirement for boys. This being so, her 'wishes' should be discounted. Ceding to the request would mean capitulating to a misogynist culture.

Saharso notes the danger in this way of approaching the issue. In most circumstances where a woman requests an abortion, she is responding in some way to social constraints: perhaps to the difficulties in her society of bringing up a child in poverty, or without a partner; perhaps to the difficulties in her society of combining motherhood with a career. That she might have reached a different decision had the circumstances been more favourable is not, on the whole, taken as invalidating her choice. Why, then, is the decision treated as less authentically 'hers' when she is responding to the difficulties in her social/cultural group of having another girl? There seems to be a rather shaky distinction here between choosing not to have another child because the social inequalities of contemporary capitalism mean the family will be condemned to poverty (regarded as a sad but legitimate choice); and choosing not to have another *girl* child because the gender inequalities of one's culture mean the family will be condemned to poverty (an unacceptable capitulation to misogyny). The point – for both Saharso and myself – is not that sex-selective abortion is fine. But it is problematic to make the case against it depend on denying the moral agency of women from minority cultures, on denying the validity of women's consent.

This, then, is the worry. Forced marriage is an undoubted harm. Initiatives to prevent it should not focus exclusively on instances that involve the use of physical force, but should address the many other ways in which pressure can be exerted on people to extract a semblance of consent. Public authorities clearly have a responsibility to assist citizens who have been kidnapped, tricked into travelling overseas or held under house arrest until they 'agree' to a marriage; and there has been promising action on this front in recent years in the UK, India, Bangladesh and Pakistan. Public authorities also have a responsibility to address the more covert instances of forced marriage, cases where the agreement is extracted through months of emotional blackmail, from young people who can see no other way out. The difficulty is that extending the initiative in this way seems to depend on querying the status of 'consent', and could easily encourage a wholesale denial of the moral agency of people from minority cultural groups. Imagine the subsequent scenario, with each and every minority 'choice' scrutinized for the over-weening power of culture, and each and every arranged marriage brought under public suspicion. In a political context that is all too ready to contrast the liberated individualism of the West with the oppressive closure of the Rest, this threatens a disturbing hierarchy of cultures.

Pateman on property in the person

The argument Carole Pateman develops in *The Sexual Contract* is illuminating here, for it offers an alternative way of querying the validity of the marriage contract that does not rely on denying the capacity to consent. As noted above, Pateman distinguishes between the conditions under which a contract is entered into (where one party might be under immense pressure to agree to unfavourable terms) and the possibly exploitative nature of the contract once it has been made. Where others have focused on the first, she is more interested in the second. Drawing inspiration from Marx's analysis of the wage contract, she argues that even the fairest of contracts can still be exploitative, if its very purpose is to establish a relationship of subordination. As lawyers will tell you, the point at which a contract bites is the point where it commits you to something you no longer wish to do. Up till then, there is no need for a contract: you happily do what the other wishes, perhaps because it is also what you wish, perhaps because you think it the right thing to do. It is when the action becomes less voluntary that the existence of the contract matters, and that is when it becomes apparent that the contract establishes a relationship of power. As Marx put it in a famous passage from *Capital* where he shifts our attention from the sphere of exchange to that of production, 'a certain change takes place, or so it appears, in the physiognomy of the *dramatis personae*'. What had earlier been 'a very Eden of the innate rights of man', with buyer and seller contracting as free and equal persons, now becomes a relationship of subordination: 'He who was previously the money-owner now strides out in front as a capitalist; the possessor of labour-power follows as his worker. The one smirks self-importantly and is intent on business; the other is timid and holds back, like someone who has brought his own hide to market and now has nothing else to expect but – a tanning.'[15] As Pateman describes it, this kind of contract establishes a condition of *civil subordination*, for what we have 'freely' given up is some of our power to govern ourselves.

In her analysis, the exploitation built into the contract is particularly stark when the contract involves property in the person – '[c]ontracts about property in the person inevitably create subordination'[16] – and much of the subsequent discussion of her work has revolved around this.[17] Some have raised doubts about her analysis of the prostitution contract, and the suggestion that it is impossible to separate out the sale of sexual services from the sale of the body itself. They have argued that treating the prostitute as engaged in something intrinsically different from others who sell their 'bodily services' – the dancer, the night-club singer or, in Martha Nussbaum's odd example, the professor of philosophy[18] – helps sustain the social stigma surrounding prostitution, and thereby the exploitative conditions under which prostitutes work. Others have taken issue with the critique of the surrogate motherhood contract as extending to women 'the masculine conception of the individual as owner, and the conception of freedom as the capacity to do what you will with your own', and thereby sweeping away 'any intrinsic relation between the female owner, her body and reproductive capacities'.[19] This has been felt to buy into a sentimentalized notion of woman as peculiarly bound up with her body, in ways that exaggerate the differences between women and men. Oddly, many of the criticisms depend on a point Pateman herself makes central to her argument: that what is true of prostitution or surrogate motherhood is also true of any kind of waged work. The curious mis-reading is revealing, for it confirms how difficult it has become for people to think of contract per se as bad.

Pateman does stress that the peculiar twist to the prostitution or surrogate motherhood contract is that the body is not just incidental but the whole point of the deal; and she argues that this marks them out as different from the standard wage-labour contract, which requires a body, but is only really concerned with the services that body performs. There is some suggestion here that men want power, not just over women, but specifically over their bodies. In other parts of *The Sexual Contract*, there is also some suggestion that women are bound up in their bodies in ways that differ from men. But, in most ways, Pateman's analysis of 'body-contracts' follows the contours of Marx's analysis of wage labour, making similar points about the impossibility of separating out any worker from his/her services. As she puts it in a later essay, 'A worker cannot send along capacities or services by themselves to an employer. The worker has to be present in the workplace if the capacities are to be "employed", to be put to use.'[20] The point, as I understand it, is not that contracts regarding marriage, prostitution and surrogate motherhood are qualitatively different from any other kind of contract, because of some weird way in which women (but only women) relate to their bodies and selves. The point is that *all* contracts regarding property in the person (hence, also, all wage-labour contracts) involve handing oneself over to someone else's power.

This perception that freedom is not only about the conditions on which we enter an agreement, but also about what kind of agreement it is, provides the extra dimension needed to address the issue of forced marriage. When attention is focused exclusively on the conditions under which people agree to marry (the more familiar way in which critics query the freedom of contract), we seem to face an unhappy choice between condoning as voluntary a number of marriages that ought to be regarded as forced, or discounting as inauthentic the supposed consent of individuals from minority cultural groups. Either we restrict the category of forced marriage to the dramas of overt compulsion (thereby denying public assistance to those who suffer 'only' from emotional blackmail); or we regard all arranged marriages with suspicion, all young women from minority cultural groups as victims, and refuse to consider them as moral agents. This second route reeks of cultural hierarchy. If we take it, moreover, it becomes hard to develop a consistent critique of cultural defence.

Drawing our attention to the content of the contract as well as the conditions under which it is entered, Pateman offers a way forward from these dilemmas. The crucial point about marriage is that it falls into that category of agreement in which individuals concede some element of personal, bodily, autonomy. It is not a one-off agreement ('I'll swap you this for that'); nor an agreement whose performance can be delegated to somebody else ('I'm sorry, I can't after all drive you to the airport, but I'll pay for a taxi instead'). Marriage is a contract involving property in the person, and as such requires your presence in order for the contract to be fulfilled. This is why the right to divorce is so important, for while we may think people should continue to be bound to a promise to pay us $1 million even when they no longer find it so convenient, this is of a different order from being bound to share someone's life, home and bed even when you no longer love or respect them. It is also, I suggest, why 'reluctant' agreement is particularly problematic in the case of marriage. If I reluctantly agree to sell my house for less than I feel it is worth – perhaps because circumstances make it impossible for me to wait for another buyer – the reluctance does not give me the right to turn up on what is now your doorstep and tell you the deal is off. Reluctantly agreeing to marry is of a different order, for, while the reluctance may dissolve after marriage (and many people do talk of how they came to know and respect their partners after marriage, not before), marriage is not the sort of contract that should be based on reluctant consent.

This is graphically illustrated in the advice given by the UK's Forced Marriage Unit to young people who fear they are about to be taken abroad for marriage purposes. Though anxious enough to have contacted the Unit for advice on what to do, many remain reluctant to cause a rift in their family by refusing to join them on the proposed trip; and they often decide to swallow their anxieties, and just trust that the fears are misplaced. Staff counselling them sometimes make the point that if they do find themselves forced into marriage, they will thereby find themselves exposed to rape, for agreement to marry will be taken as agreement to sex, and may well end up with agreement to become a mother. This is a very Pateman-like point. It relies on the fact that a contract to marry is an unusual kind of contract, dealing with property in the person. As such, it is the kind of contract that hands *you* (not your money or car or house) over into someone else's power.

Domestic violence is more vigorously pursued by the police than was the case when *The Sexual Contract* was first published, and marital rape is more widely recognized as a prosecutable offence. In many legal jurisdictions, divorce is more readily available and divorce settlements have become more equitable; indeed, in quite a few jurisdictions, men now complain that they are treated less well than women. Women have more protections within marriage, and find it easier, on the whole, to leave, and the loss of autonomy associated with an agreement to marry has been correspondingly reduced. It would be risky, however, to exaggerate the implications of this, and excessively optimistic to suggest that the marriage contract no longer involves any relationship of power. Like an agreement to work for someone, an agreement to marry involves suspending some of the powers of self-government. Focusing only on the moment of consent (was it free or forced?) is therefore particularly misleading when it comes to marriage, for we also need to take account of the kind of agreement that marriage entails. I noted earlier that we would not want to invalidate every decision arrived at under emotional or financial pressure, and asked what, if anything, marks out decisions regarding marriage as different. Well, perhaps it is this. Agreeing to marry is not just any old agreement. It is an agreement to give up on some of your future freedom to decide for yourself.

Pateman says at one point that '[a] free social order cannot be a contractual order'.[21] I have never been entirely sure how to take this: as an encouragement to create a social order with no contracts at all, to create a social order with no contracts in the person, or as a reminder that freedom is always under threat in a contractual order, and needs to be underpinned by a strong democracy in order to keep the dangers at bay? Whichever interpretation one adopts, she is surely right to point out the fallacy of contract: the false belief that if you have freely agreed, you cannot then say that fulfilling the contract makes you unfree. There may be cases where this once-and-for-all agreement is plausible, but not that of marriage. Pateman's critique of the marriage and other 'body contracts' then provides us, I think, with some of what we need to differentiate the kind of agreement necessary to marriage from other kinds of agreement. In doing so, it helps us avoid the pitfalls in discussions of forced and arranged marriage, and, specifically, the suggestion that the 'consent' of a young Muslim, Hindu or Sikh is less valid than the consent of a young Christian, atheist or Jew. The point about forced marriage is not just that people are forced into it, but that what they are forced into is marriage. Public authorities need to act decisively against forced marriage, and this means recognizing emotional as well as physical coercion, and protecting individuals from both. But the extra vigilance required in relation to marriage is dictated by the nature of the marriage contract, not by a lesser capacity for decision-making among individuals from minority cultural groups.

8

Consent, autonomy and coercion: forced marriage, public policy and the courts

Forced marriage is an abuse of human rights, and can involve people in years of misery and violence. There is no question that governments have a responsibility to intervene effectively against it. There seem, however, to be a number of obstacles that get in the way of effective intervention; I explore these in this chapter, drawing on the example of UK policy and legal cases from the British courts.

The first problem is that any defensible policy regarding forced marriage must start from a distinction between arranged and forced, yet the distinction rests on complicated interpretations of freedom and consent that do not lend themselves to simple rules. Some people, of course, reject the distinction entirely, and think it unacceptable when there is *any* kind of parental involvement in the search for appropriate marriage partners. This was, until recently, the presumption in the Danish approach to forced marriage, where policy pronouncements rarely distinguished between a consensual arranged marriage and one that involves coercion, and where 'arranged' and 'forced' were treated as interchangeable terms. If this is one's view, the only important distinction will be between love marriage and *any* kind of arranged/forced marriage, with all the latter regarded as a denial of personal autonomy. I do not share this perspective. In my view, it under-estimates the extent of parental involvement in supposed love marriages, where there may be considerable pressure not to get involved with partners perceived as inappropriate by virtue of their social class, skin colour, religion or, of course, gender. It reduces the seriousness of being forced into an unwanted marriage by placing it on a par with arranged ones. And it under-estimates the often voluntary participation of young people in arranged marriages, and their support for a system that might plausibly promise greater compatibility of spouses than chance meetings on a dance floor or in a crowded bar. The easy dismissal of arranged marriage invokes a familiar binary of modern versus traditional, and conveys an arrogant lack of respect for difference.

The more serious criticism is that arranged marriage treats marriage primarily as a social institution rather than a relationship between individuals. It then becomes vulnerable to the complaints sometimes levelled at campaigners for same-sex marriage, whose efforts to extend the benefits of marriage beyond the heterosexual couple are seen as contributing to the institution's social mystique and power. I have some sympathy for this criticism, which is, of course, a critique of marriage per se. I also think arranged marriage tends to institutionalize further what is already too prevalent in social behaviour, the tendency, that is, to select partners exclusively from among one's 'own kind'. But if multiculturalism is to mean anything, it must mean recognizing that there are many different ways of organizing one's life, and that no one person or group has a monopoly on what is right. It is worth adding – though this is a more pragmatic point – that initiatives against forced marriage are most effective when they gain support from within the communities where arranged marriage is most practised and forced marriage most likely to occur. Such support is easier to achieve when governments give a clear indication that initiatives against forced marriage are *not* intended as attacks on arranged marriage.

We need, therefore, some such distinction, yet the basis for it is highly suspect. In the starker cases that lend themselves most readily to criminal prosecution – cases where parents or other family members have kidnapped an under-age girl, taken her out of the country and held her in captivity until she 'agrees' to the marriage – it is easy enough to identify the coercion. But if we make the distinction too sharp, we find ourselves forced on to crude measures of physical coercion. If we make it too soft, we may end up denying the possibility of a genuinely consensual arranged marriage. The arranged/forced distinction revolves around complex issues in the definition and understanding of consent, with a large grey area in between.

This is further complicated by the second problem, which relates to the uses and abuses of culture. The notion that 'my culture made me do it' is not normally seen as the appropriate response when someone is charged with violence against women or the brutal treatment of a child, and even the strongest supporters of multiculturalism will criticize the uses and abuses of culture in matters of criminal defence. Some people will say it *is* indeed 'in the culture' to behave like that, but consider this no excuse for violent behaviour. Others take issue with such ways of describing a culture, arguing that one cannot say of *any* culture that it prescribes only one possible course of action, and that all cultures contain a diversity of practices and views. Others criticize what they see as the false opposition between acting as an individual agent and succumbing to social and cultural influence, noting that agency only becomes possible through social context, and cannot then be represented as incompatible with social influence. As I have argued elsewhere, an objectification of culture that makes it appear as if 'cultures' act, not people, is thoroughly misleading. People are *not* defined by their cultures; cultural difference is much exaggerated; and there can be as much variation in beliefs and behaviour within what are conceived as cultural groups as between them. Much of the talk about culture and cultural practices is little more than cultural stereotyping.

The complication is that, in legal cases relating to forced marriage, the more sensitive judgments have generally been those that operate with a strong conception of cultural difference and take cultural considerations into account. In annulment cases, for example, judges are assessing whether a marriage is invalidated by evidence that one party or the other was coerced into it, or was a genuine marriage from which people are now trying to extricate themselves. The stigma of divorce weighs more heavily in some communities than others (this itself implies significant cultural difference); and while the high costs associated with bringing a case for annulment make it unlikely that many people would opt for this over applying for a divorce, there might still be reasons falsely to represent a valid marriage as forced. The key issue in annulment cases is therefore whether the representation of a particular marriage as forced is convincing. Rulings in the earliest cases tended to tackle this with a pretty blunt instrument.

British courts operated for a number of years with what they described (after the judge in question) as the Simon test. If you were threatened with the loss of life, liberty or limb, or if it was reasonable for you to think you were in danger of losing any of these, then you could be said to be acting under duress. Anything short of this was held not to count – at least, not until the courts began to take cultural considerations more into account. It was only when judges began to acknowledge that it is harder for young people to stand up to parental pressure where there is a strong expectation of deference to elders, or that a threat to disown will be particularly threatening where personal identity is closely bound up with family and community ties, that the judgments became more nuanced. An increased engagement with cultural difference thus delivered a more context-sensitive understanding of consent, in ways that I mostly applaud. But where then should one draw the line between a culturally sensitive practice of legal judgment (thought to be good) and culture as excuse (usually perceived as bad)?

The third problem – all too familiar from the terrain of gender and culture – is that initiatives to address harms against women from minority cultural groups can end up fuelling cultural stereotypes and strengthening prejudice against minority groups. To repeat: forced marriage is an abuse of human rights, and governments have a responsibility to act against it. But policies to address the problem have not focused exclusively on preventing that harm. Governments have often ignored what might seem the most obvious measures, like funding women's groups that have been helping people out of forced marriages for years, or funding refuges for those who have to flee family homes to escape a marriage. Sidestepping measures that involve money and active support, governments have turned to modifications of immigration rules instead. Controlling the entry of 'dubious' spouses has frequently doubled as a way of reducing the incidence of forced marriage and reducing the impact on immigration figures of family reunification policies. Indeed, one might say it has served three distinct functions. Some politicians and opinion formers (including former UK Home Secretary David Blunkett) have argued that people should be discouraged from forming the transcontinental marriages through which former migrants retain their links with countries of origin, and be persuaded to throw in their lot entirely with their new country. Depending on how the issue of forced marriage is framed, public concern about the rights and protections of vulnerable young people then risks becoming a proxy for restrictions on immigration, and assimilationist pressures on minority groups. The main effect of what might otherwise be desirable initiatives may be to demonize minority groups rather than improve the condition of young people within them.

In the case of the UK, there is no doubt that policy on forced marriage has suffered from its entanglement with immigration issues. It is notable, for example, that the coyly named Community Liaison Unit, set up in 2000 to deal with the issue and later re-launched as the Forced Marriage Unit, was physically housed in the Foreign and Commonwealth Office. The Home Office, which generally tackles matters of abuse or domestic violence, might have seemed the more natural home. It is also notable that the unit focused its activities on what was called the 'overseas dimension', taking as its remit the protection of people from coercion into marriage with spouses from abroad, and offering little beyond advice to those forced into marriage with other UK citizens.[1] Government officials became increasingly interested in the 2002 Danish initiative which had set a minimum age of twenty-four for marriage partners entering Denmark from outside the European Union or Nordic countries; and the UK government introduced a regulation in 2003 that refused entry clearance to overseas spouses until both parties to the marriage were at least eighteen. In 2008, after public consultation, and some government-funded research that recommended *against* further raising of this minimum, the government raised the bar higher to twenty-one. Not surprisingly, the deployment of forced marriage in measures that reduce or delay immigration has generated suspicions about the real agenda.

Some of the policies developed arguably put women at *more* risk of harm. In 2003, for example, the government introduced a two-year probationary period for people entering the country on the basis of marriage to a person settled in the UK. Up till then, spouses could apply in their own right for indefinite leave to remain after one year in the country. The doubling to a two-year minimum was framed by worries about 'bogus' marriages: having to live with your spouse for only a year was seen as offering too easy a route to residency. But the tightening of what was perceived in official circles as a loophole in immigration regulations proved particularly problematic for women in abusive marriages (and where a marriage *is* forced on unwilling participants, the chances that it might also involve abuse are arguably higher). Where it is the woman who is the UK citizen, she is likely to face enormous pressure to remain in the marriage for the necessary two years so as to give her spouse residency rights. If she is the one brought into the UK as a spouse, she faces deportation to her country of origin, possibly even persecution for having abandoned the marriage, should she decide to leave a violent spouse. Under pressure from minority women's groups, the government later agreed that a woman who proves marital breakdown because of violence can apply for residency rights before the full two years – the so-called 'domestic violence concession'. The standard of proof has, however, been set high, and she has no access to public funds while her application is pending. Many activists feel this failure to support women exposed to violent and abusive marriages, and the seemingly overwhelming preoccupation with closing immigration loopholes, gives the lie to official claims about wanting to protect women from abuse.[2]

The tension between supporting vulnerable young people and demonizing cultural groups is perhaps best illustrated through the issue of legislation, and whether the government should pass a law specifically banning forced marriage. Introducing specific legislation on forced marriage is mostly a red herring: pretty much all countries already have laws against coercion, and most additionally signed up to international conventions that specify that marriage must be based on free consent. When the Working Group on Forced Marriage (the first official body charged with addressing the issue) reported in 2000, it noted that forced marriage had long been illegal in Britain, and could be prosecuted under any number of existing laws, including those against kidnapping, child abduction, false imprisonment, assault, battery, threats to kill, harassment and blackmail.[3] The Home Office nonetheless returned to the issue five years later with a consultation paper on the introduction of a law making it a crime to force someone to marry.[4] The revival of the issue reflects the hardening line against multiculturalism, and belief that previous measures had not sent a sufficiently clear message about the unacceptability of forced marriage. It also chimed with the introduction of the Female Genital Mutilation Act 2003, an almost entirely symbolic piece of legislation that updated an equally symbolic Prohibition of Female Circumcision Act 1985, without providing any significant additional funding to organizations addressing the problem. In both cases, legislation seems more designed to point the finger of blame at particular cultural communities than to eradicate harms to women. When a problem is singled out as a 'practice' of particular minority groups, and treated as if it were entirely separate from other problems of abuse, coercion or violence, this establishes it as a problem of 'culture', rather than of family or spousal violence.

In the event, the majority of responses to the forced marriage consultation were opposed to the legislation, with some division of opinion among the NGOs most active in this field, and perhaps unexpected opposition from the police. The government subsequently announced that it would not proceed with legislation, because the necessary legal tools already existed, there was no reason to think that a new law would lead to any significant increase in prosecutions, and it might be seen as unfairly targeting particular minority groups. A Forced Marriage (Civil Protection) Act was passed in 2007, but this followed a private member's bill introduced by Lord Lester, a leading human rights lawyer, and dealt in civil remedies rather than criminal law. It received government backing. In a useful recognition of the importance of employing generic, rather than culture-specific legislation, it eventually passed into law as an amendment to the

Family Law Act (1996). The Act allows the person seeking protection, or a third party acting on his/her behalf, to apply for a forced marriage protection order, which can then be used to prevent actions likely to lead to a forced marriage. In effect, it clarifies and further enables what had already developed as case law, including through some of the cases discussed below. On past practice, protection orders are likely to include requiring people to deliver a person thought to be under house arrest to a safe place where s/he can be interviewed to establish her/his wishes, or confiscating the passports of family members to prevent them taking a person abroad for marriage. Anyone breaching an order will be liable for arrest.

More could be said about the evolution of public policy, but I want to turn at this point to the legal cases, for it is through these that questions of agency, autonomy and consent have been most fully explored. UK policy on forced marriage (though not always the pronouncements of politicians) has been characterized by a clear distinction between arranged and forced, with the evident intention of avoiding the kind of demonization discussed above. Policy then operates as if there is no great difficulty in making this distinction. The explanation given in the first major statement is reiterated in virtually every subsequent official document: 'In the tradition of arranged marriages . . . [t]he spouses have the right to choose – to say no – at any time. In forced marriage, there is no choice.'[5] This same distinction figures in the legal cases. In *NS* v. *MI* (2006), for example, the judgment opens with the declaration that 'arranged marriages are perfectly lawful', not in any way to be condemned, but 'to be supported as a conventional concept in many societies'. It contrasts these with forced marriages, described as 'intolerable', an 'abomination' and a 'gross abuse of human rights'.[6] There is, then, no obvious difference between politicians and judges as regards the official distinction, but it is through the legal judgments that questions of what constitutes agency and consent have been most fully explored and the meanings of coercion refined. I turn now to these.

The legal cases

Criminal prosecutions

The legal cases fall under four main categories: criminal prosecutions (virtually none); petitions in the civil courts for the annulment of a marriage on the grounds of lack of consent; wardship proceedings to protect people who might otherwise be forced into marriage; and the use of civil remedies for such torts as trespass to the person and false imprisonment. There are few criminal cases relating to forced marriage, not because of a lack of specific legislation criminalizing forced marriage, but because the victims of the crime are mostly unwilling to co-operate in taking a criminal action against the perpetrators. These are, typically, close members of their own family, very often their parents, and it is only in cases of extreme violence and/or where family relations have irrevocably broken down that victims are prepared to see their parents imprisoned. In the case of *R* v. *Ghulam Rasool* (1990–1), which involved the use of force to prevent a marriage rather than promote one, a step-father was charged with kidnapping his step-daughter to prevent her marrying a non-Muslim.[7] At the trial, the young woman said she was reconciled with her family and wanted neither Rasool nor his co-accused (her mother and brothers) prosecuted. The case continued, and Rasool was convicted and sentenced to two years' imprisonment; but one can imagine the reluctance of public prosecutors to pursue cases when key witnesses might later withdraw.

It is often said that a few well-publicized criminal prosecutions would do much to deter families from forcing their children into marriage, but the self-evident difficulties in pursuing cases through to conclusion make this a rare occurrence. In one much-publicized but not prosecuted case in 2008, Dr Humayra Abedin, a trainee National Health Service doctor in her early thirties, travelled to Bangladesh on hearing that her mother was ill, and then seemingly disappeared. It was feared that her parents were trying to force her into marriage in order to end her relationship with a man they regarded as unacceptable. Using the provisions of the Forced Marriage (Civil Protection) Act, a High Court judge in London passed an order requiring her return to the UK. This was not enforceable in Bangladesh, but a High Court in Dhaka also ordered her parents to return her passport, driver's licence and credit card, and to allow Dr Abedin to appear before it. The family gave way, Dr Abedin returned to London, but insisted that she had no bad feelings towards her parents. As she put it in a television interview, 'They are my parents so I don't have any bad feelings.' There has been no prosecution.

Annulment cases

The annulment cases, by definition, involve marriages that have taken place, and it is through these that the meanings of coercion and consent have been most obviously refined. Up until the early 1980s, the Simon test largely set the terms: petitioners seeking the annulment of a marriage had to establish that they had entered it under duress, and duress was interpreted as reasonably held fear of physical harm.[8] This translated into some pretty unsympathetic judgments. In *Singh* v. *Singh* (1971), the Court of Appeal refused a decree of nullity to a seventeen-year-old Sikh girl who had been through a civil marriage ceremony but later refused to confirm it through a religious ceremony or have anything to do with her husband.[9] The judges decided she would have been willing enough to continue with the marriage had the man in question been (as promised) handsome and educated. In what now seems an extraordinary trivialization of her situation, they concluded that when she saw him for the first time 'she did not like what she saw', and therefore changed her mind after the ceremony. Despite her age, her obvious vulnerability to parental pressure, and the fact that the two young people had not met before the ceremony, this was accepted as a marriage based on free consent.

The turning point came with *Hirani* v. *Hirani* (1983), which involved a nineteen-year-old Hindu woman who went through both civil and religious ceremonies but left the (unconsummated) marriage after six weeks.[10] The court refused a decree of nullity, but in this case her application was allowed on appeal. The decision established a new definition of duress that no longer revolved around threats of physical violence: the crucial question was 'whether the mind of the applicant (the victim) has in fact been overborne, howsoever that was caused'. The case was described as 'as clear a case as one could want of the overbearing of the will of the petitioner and thus invalidating or vitiating her consent'.

Nullity proceedings are expensive, so not a remedy available to all, and in recent cases some judges have called for public funds to be made available to enable such proceedings.[11] But where cases have been brought, the courts have worked with the wider understanding of what it is to have one's consent invalidated, and have further extended its remit. In *Mahmood* v. *Mahmood* (1993), one of a number of important judgments from the Scottish courts, the parents had threatened to cut off financial support and send the young woman to live in Pakistan if she refused to go ahead with the marriage. She was twenty-one at the time and working in her parents' shop. Since both her elder sister and brother had already been disowned after refusing arranged marriages, the threats must have seemed very real. Rejecting the notion that it was necessary to establish fear of physical violence, the judge noted that these 'could be regarded as matters which could have overridden the will of a girl of her age and cultural background'.[12] Note here some of the difficulties regarding the use of 'culture'. Taking cultural background into account provided a more sensitive reading of the pressures to which the young woman was subjected, leading, in my view, to a better judgment; but it relied, at the same time, on a suggestion that young women of her 'cultural background' would be less capable than young women of other backgrounds of deciding and acting for themselves.

Men, too, have benefited from a context-dependent understanding of coercion, though I am inclined to think the judgment in *Mahmud* v. *Mahmud* (1994) lends itself to a more cynical interpretation. This involved a thirty-year-old man, living apart from his family and not financially dependent on them, who had been made to believe that his persistent refusal to marry had brought about his father's death, and was bringing shame and degradation on his family. The judge argued that, in cases of moral pressure, there was 'no general basis for expecting the male to be stronger than the female or the thirty-year-old to be less swayed by conscience than the twenty-four-year-old', and granted a decree of nullity.[13] In this case, the man had been living for some years with a non-Muslim woman; they had one child and were expecting another; and the cousin brought over from Pakistan for the marriage had already been deported at the time of the case. Wrapping things up with a decree of nullity may have seemed the best course of action in these circumstances – but did the judge *really* mean that the will of a financially independent thirty-year-old can be overridden by his mother's persistent guilt-tripping? In these cases, what is presumed to be the culture of close-knit South Asian families, with a strong sense of what is owed to family honour, is felt to heighten vulnerability to parental pressure and make it harder for young people to resist moral blackmail. This is an advance on the harsh *Singh* v. *Singh* judgment, but arguably allows too much latitude to cultural stereotyping, and can lead to the infantilization of young women and men.

Wardship proceedings

The earlier wardship proceedings dealt with people under the age of maturity (eighteen in the UK), so it is perhaps less appropriate to complain of infantilization in these cases. However, their subsequent evolution – first, to deal with adults made vulnerable by reasons of mental or physical disability, and, with the passage of the Forced Marriage (Civil Protection) Act, potentially to any adult – definitely raises this issue. Wardship proceedings have been used in innovative ways to protect potential victims of forced marriage since the influential *Re KR* (1999).[14] This involved a seventeen-year-old Sikh girl who was taken to the Punjab and placed in the custody of relatives pending her marriage. Her sister – who had herself left home to avoid an unwanted marriage – successfully applied to have her made a ward of court, and the judge drew up an order requiring co-operation in returning her to the UK. With the aid of this, KR was able to persuade her relatives to take her to the British High Commission in Delhi, where she was interviewed to establish her wishes, and flown home. This case is, with reason, regarded as exemplary, demonstrating an effective use of the courts in providing much-needed protection. Later cases raise more complex issues about who has the authority to decide.

In *Re M Minors* (2003), the same judge (Singer) directed a local authority to consider making an application for a care order so as to protect two orphaned girls of Pakistani origin, aged thirteen and fifteen at the time of the hearing, who had been taken to Pakistan after the death of their father, and had seemingly gone through betrothal ceremonies there.[15] Intervention by the Foreign Office resulted in their repatriation to the UK, where they were placed with a foster carer. The judge was concerned that the girls' expressed wishes (presumably to return to where they had been living in the UK) might leave them still vulnerable to family pressures, hence that they might benefit from the additional legal protection of being subject to a care order. This was probably a justified concern, but the case still raises difficult questions (familiar, of course, from wider questions about the protection of young people and the age at which they can be said to make decisions for themselves) about when and where public authorities should intervene to protect what are perceived as vulnerable young people. The questions become more difficult still when the legal process is employed for those over the age of maturity, as has increasingly been the case in recent years.

In the unusual case of *SK* (2004), a solicitor with extensive expertise in abduction and forced marriage cases (she was involved in *KR*, and the *Abedin* case) applied on behalf of the proposed plaintiff for a court order requiring family members to bring her to the British High Commission in Dhaka for an interview to establish her wishes.

The woman in question was an adult British citizen, thought to be detained in Bangladesh against her will, but not herself involved in starting the legal proceedings. The case is an important one, because it established a precedent for employing court orders to protect adults (those over eighteen) as well as children. The order was granted; SK was interviewed in Dhaka, and did return home; but 'conveyed her wish that the proceedings should not continue, maintaining that she had no need of the court's intervention on her behalf'.[16] Without more detailed knowledge, it is hard to guess at what was going on here. It may be that the court was too ready to assume someone was at risk of a forced marriage when in fact she was merely visiting relatives. But it is also entirely plausible that the young woman *was* at risk, and continued to be so, but that her family successfully pressured her into denying any problem. The case recalls the many obstacles in the way of achieving criminal convictions for forced marriage, when these typically depend on children giving evidence against their parents. It also reinforces the difficult balance between acting on what could be ill-founded – possibly stereotypical – assumptions, and failing to give adequate protection.

In other cases where protections already established for children have been extended to adults, there has been an issue of mental or physical capacity. This has been a growing area of concern: the Forced Marriage Unit reported in 2007 that around 80 of the 400 cases they had dealt with in the previous year involved adults or school-age people with learning difficulties. Reading through some of the reported cases, it looks as if families sometimes turn to an arranged (but is it then forced?) marriage as the solution for family members with learning difficulties, seeing this as offering a better life than the institutional care that might otherwise be the alternative when the parents themselves die. The intention may be protective, but the risks of abuse are high, and social workers have been concerned as to whether the individuals involved really are giving their consent.

The case of *SA*, for example, involved a profoundly deaf young woman, who also had learning difficulties, and had been taught to communicate in English Sign Language; since English was not the main language spoken in her family, she had no real medium of communication at home.[17] She had turned eighteen, and had indicated that she wanted to marry and was happy to go to Pakistan for the purposes of an arranged marriage. She was also very clear that she then wanted to return to England and live with her husband in her home town. The local authority was concerned that SA was vulnerable to manipulation, and that her limited communication meant she was not in a position to give her informed consent. They were particularly worried that she might find herself living in Pakistan pending her spouse's application for entry to the UK, with no way of communicating with those around her, and none of her existing forms of support.

The outcome of the proceedings was eminently sensible, and demonstrated considerable respect for SA's agency. The court drew up an order requiring her written consent, translated and explained in sign language, before her parents would be permitted to apply for her travel documents or to arrange a marriage. It also required written consent from the prospective spouse that she would be enabled to return home within four months, even if his immigration status had not yet been resolved. The judge went to considerable lengths to affirm respect for arranged marriage, and relied mainly on precedents from medical cases (rather than cultural ones) in deciding to extend to an adult protections usually restricted to minors. The wider significance of the case is the way it extends the scope for legal intervention to protect 'a vulnerable adult, who, even if not incapacitated by mental illness or disorder, is, or is reasonably believed to be, either (i) under constraint or (ii) subject to coercion or undue influence or (iii) for some other reason deprived of the capacity to make the relevant decision'.[18] Culture features strongly here, particularly in the judge's elaboration of coercion or undue influence. He notes that influence can be particularly insidious when it is 'that of a parent or other close or dominating relative, and where the arguments and persuasion are based upon personal affection or duty, religious beliefs, powerful social or cultural conventions, or asserted social, familial or domestic obligation'. There is an implied contrast here between majority (presumed to be secular, individualist and with weak cultural conventions) and minority (presumed to be religious, family oriented and culturally driven or defined).

As in the annulment cases, there is a difficult balance to be achieved, between a culturally sensitive appreciation of the kinds of pressures that can be put on people by the immediate and wider family, and a culturally stereotyped representation of people as less capable of agency or choice. There is evidence of some careful thinking about the need to avoid cultural stereotypes – yet stereotypes still creep in. In *Re K* (2005), Justice Munby (the same judge as in *SA*) refused a local authority application for an order to protect the sixteen-year-old daughter of Iraqi Kurds from an early marriage. In this case, the social workers were anxious that the young woman was too young to know her own mind, and was being unduly pressured to follow what her parents considered appropriate. Here, too, Munby took issue with the social workers' account, and stressed the young woman's capacity for choice. In his judgment he said:

> We must guard against the risk of stereotyping. We must be careful to ensure that our understandable concern to protect vulnerable children (or, indeed, vulnerable young adults) does not lead us to interfere inappropriately – and if inappropriately then unjustly – with families merely because they cleave, as this family does, to mores, to cultural beliefs, more or less different from what is familiar to those who view life from a purely Euro-centric perspective. It would be a tragic irony if the full weight of the wardship jurisdiction was to be deployed against those sections of our community who, paying particular regard to the importance of marriage and the unacceptability of pre-marital sexual relations, tend for that very reason to marry young, whilst leaving untouched those sections of our community who, treating pre-marital sexual relations and co-habitation without the benefit of matrimony as almost the norm, tend for that reason not to marry until they are well into their twenties.[19]

While the declared intent is to reject the tendency to stereotype, the comment seems to invoke two stereotypical accounts of two different 'sections of our community'. It is also striking that, while annulment cases have regarded people under twenty-one as particularly susceptible to coercion – and immigration regulations now regard twenty-one as the age of maturity for choosing a spouse from outside the EU – the judgment in this case recognizes a sixteen-year-old as capable of knowing her own mind.

In *MAB* v. *City Council* (again, dealt with by Munby), a local authority applied for an injunction to prevent the marriage of a twenty-five-year old man with a severe autistic disorder to a cousin in Pakistan. The family had been trying to arrange this marriage for a number of years in the hope of providing more securely for his future and with what seemed the full co-operation of the cousin. In the opinion of two psychiatrists, however, MAB did not sufficiently understand the nature and responsibilities of marriage or sexual relations to give his consent. In deciding the case, the judge again stressed the importance of avoiding cultural stereotypes; accepted the undertaking of the parents that they now recognized the unsuitability of marriage for their son and would not cause or permit one; and required the local authority to pay two-thirds of the parents' costs because its insistence on pressing for injunctions rather than undertakings had (in his judgment) unnecessarily prolonged the proceedings.

It is clear from such cases that legal proceedings can operate as an important protection against coercion or abuse. Yet in some, the courts are arguably over-zealous in protecting people from presumed threats. In others, they seem to provide a useful restraint on over-zealous social workers, who have been less willing than the judges to trust the parents, and more inclined to step in to protect people 'for their own good'. At their best, the courts do seem to be identifying and grappling with the right kind of issues: how to determine when people need protection, from others but also on occasion from themselves; how to determine when young or vulnerable people are able to make their own decisions; how to recognize the ways in which culture makes a difference without falling into cultural stereotype. Whether they consistently succeed in this last is more debatable.

Civil remedies

As with the criminal prosecutions, civil remedies remain a small category, though one that is likely to grow over the coming years. There are already cases of people being awarded civil damages because of harms to the person that occurred in the context of an arranged or forced marriage. In *Singh* v. *Bhakar* (2006), for example, the judge awarded £35,000 to a Sikh woman subjected to what he described as 'four months of hell' after an arranged marriage that collapsed, largely due to her treatment by her mother-in law.[20] In that case, there was no suggestion that the woman had been coerced into the marriage – the case revolved around her treatment after the ceremony – but it is likely that the law of tort will be increasingly used for claiming damages in cases of forced marriage. This, indeed, is one of the subsidiary aims of the Forced Marriage (Civil Protection) Act. While primarily concerned with clarifying and easing the process of taking out a protection order to prevent a marriage, the legislation also makes it clearer that there are civil remedies for people damaged by coercion into marriage, specifying remedies under the Protection from Harassment Act (1997) and the law of tort. It is too early to judge whether this will lead to a substantial number of cases for damages.

Conclusion

On the question of how to differentiate consensual from coerced marriage, and how to register the significance of culture without reifying cultural difference, it sometimes seems that politicians and judges are pulling in different directions. Politicians want to make it clear that their critique of forced marriage is *not* an attack on arranged marriage; and when they toy with the idea of new legislation more explicitly criminalizing forced marriage, they have the more overt forms of coercion in mind. They operate, therefore, with a rather simple notion of 'arranged marriage = consensual' versus 'forced marriage = coerced', overlooking what is inevitably a continuum. By contrast, in both annulment cases and wardship proceedings, judges have to differentiate in subtle ways what counts as emotional blackmail or manipulation, and where individuals can be said to be making up their own minds, and they no longer employ simpler notions of physical violence as the key test. Politicians also seem to have decided that no one under the age of twenty-one and of non-European descent can be said to know her own mind, but must be protected from coercion into marriage with an overseas spouse by being prevented from marrying at all.[21] Judges, by contrast, make more nuanced decisions about when a particular combination of age and 'culture' indicates ability to know what one is doing – sometimes deciding that a young woman of sixteen knows her own mind, sometimes that a man of thirty did not.

One might conclude from this that the law is a more suitable, because more subtle and precise, instrument for dealing with the complexities of coercion and consent, but that would be premature. There has, indeed, been innovative use of annulment petitions, wardship proceedings and court orders to provide greater security to those exposed to forced marriage. The legal establishment has become more responsive to people's needs and vulnerabilities, and more able to recognize the complex ways in which people can be subject to coercion, as it has become more sensitive to cultural difference. The courts have then provided an arena within which complex issues of consent have been identified and addressed. But sensitivity to cultural difference easily slides over into cultural stereotyping, and there are indications of this even in judgments that explicitly repudiate cultural stereotypes. The courts are by no means immune to cultural stereotyping, including at those moments when they explicitly disavow it. Indeed, why should we expect them to be so, when judges are overwhelmingly drawn from majority communities, and are mostly products of majority culture?

As to the greater subtlety of the law, there *is* a generic difference, particularly in the common law system of the UK where judgments may revolve around detailed interpretation of individual events, intentions, understandings and motives, and are able to engage with a level of psychological complexity that escapes the average immigration or other official. Public policy inclines to simpler generalizations, leaving only a small room for discretionary decision, while the law can differentiate more precisely between degrees of autonomy or coercion. But that is not to say we can then look to the law courts for a solution. The two most damning problems with the law as a way of tackling the problem of forced marriage are that legal remedies are costly, and that they mostly act after the event. Legal remedies are only available to those who have the time and money to pursue cases through the courts, hence the recommendations in some recent cases that public money should be made available to people pursuing annulments or applying for a court order. Annulments, moreover, do not prevent forced marriages, but only dissolve them; civil damages provide some compensation, but only after the damage has been done. The law may be a more subtle instrument, but is not going to help all that many.

If I were drawing up my list of priorities for addressing the problem of forced marriage, I would stress funding for agencies working on the ground; funding, accommodation and avenues for education or employment for those threatened with coercion or escaping a forced marriage; better training for teachers and social workers in recognizing and supporting those at risk; and more teachers and social workers with real connections to the relevant communities. This involves money, of course, and in all the talk about the need for action on forced marriage, money has remained in short supply. One of the many ironies of current policy discourse is that refuges created specifically for South Asian women, and serving, among others, those fleeing a forced marriage, are being represented as out-moded just at the time when there is more official emphasis than ever on the need to tackle the problem of forced marriage. (This is part of what provokes activist cynicism about the 'real' agenda.) The drift away from multiculturalism has brought with it a disenchantment with what is seen as 'community-specific' social provision: better by far, we are told, to have generic refuges that cater for women of all races and religions than to separate people on the basis of their religion or ethnic group. Generic legislation on domestic violence is, in my view, to be favoured over specific legislation that treats forced marriage as a culturally distinct phenomenon, and thereby cuts it off from the larger category of violence against women. But generic *refuges* are not so obviously superior to community-specific ones, at least not while we live in racist societies. As Amrit Wilson puts it, 'generic (essentially white) women's refuges neither provide for the cultural needs of South Asians nor offer a racism-free atmosphere where deeply traumatised women and children can recover'.[22] Treating the problem as specific to particular cultures but then offering mainly generic solutions seems to have it just the wrong way round.

Notes

I   GENDER AND CULTURE: INTRODUCTION

1   Including Moira Gatens, 'A Critique of the Sex/Gender Distinction', in *Beyond Marxism? Interventions after Marx*, ed. Judith Allen and Paul Patten. Sydney: Intervention Publications, 1983: 143–60; and Judith Butler, *Gender Trouble: Feminism and the Subversion of Identity*. New York and London: Routledge, 1990. For a good overview of feminist critiques of the sex/gender distinction, see Raia Prokhovnik, *Rational Woman: A Feminist Critique of Dichotomy*. Manchester: Manchester University Press, 2002.
2   Susan Moller Okin with respondents, *Is Multiculturalism Bad for Women?* ed. Joshua Cohen, Matthew Howard and Martha C. Nussbaum. Princeton, NJ: Princeton University Press, 1999: 131. For the more developed argument, see Susan Moller Okin, 'Feminism and Multiculturalism: Some Tensions', *Ethics*, 108 (1998): 661–84.
3   For a comparative analysis of this phenomenon across a number of European countries, see Anne Phillips and Sawitri Saharso (eds.), 'The Rights of Women and the Crisis of Multiculturalism', *Ethnicities*, 8/3 (2008): 291–301.
4   For the UK, see Moira Dustin and Anne Phillips, 'Whose Agenda Is It? Abuses of Women and Abuses of "Culture" in Britain', *Ethnicities*, 8/3 (2008): 405–24; and Amrit Wilson, 'The Forced Marriage Debate and the British State', *Race and Class*, 49/1 (2007): 25–38.
5   Critiques include Leti Volpp, 'Feminism and Multiculturalism', *Columbia Law Review*, 101 (2001): 1181–218; Anne Norton, 'Review Essay on Euben, Okin and Nussbaum', *Political Theory*, 29/5 (2001): 736–49; Ayelet Shachar, *Multicultural Jurisdictions: Cultural Differences and Women's Rights*. Cambridge and New York: Cambridge University Press, 2001.
6   Shachar, *Multicultural Jurisdictions*. See also Shachar, 'Feminism and Multiculturalism: Mapping the Terrain', in *Multiculturalism and*

Political Theory, ed. Anthony Simon Laden and David Owen. Cambridge and New York: Cambridge University Press, 2007: 115–47.

7   Seyla Benhabib, *The Claims of Culture: Equality and Diversity in the Global Era*. Princeton, NJ, and Oxford: Princeton University Press, 2002; Monique Deveaux, *Cultural Pluralism and Dilemmas of Justice*. Ithaca and London: Cornell University Press, 2000; Sarah Song, *Justice, Gender, and the Politics of Multiculturalism*. Cambridge: Cambridge University Press, 2007. I take the notion of cultural dissenter from Madhavi Sunder, 'Cultural Dissent', *Stanford Law Review*, 54 (2001): 495–567.

8   Uma Narayan, *Dislocating Cultures: Identities, Traditions, and Third World Feminism*. London and New York: Routledge, 1997; Narayan, 'Essence of Culture and a Sense of History: A Feminist Critique of Cultural Essentialism', *Hypatia*, 13/2 (1998): 86–106; Leti Volpp, 'Talking "Culture": Gender, Race, Nation and the Politics of Multiculturalism', *Columbia Law Review*, 96/6 (1996): 1573–617; Monique Deveaux, *Gender and Justice in Multicultural Liberal States*. Oxford and New York: Oxford University Press, 2008.

9   Anne Phillips, *Multiculturalism without Culture*. Princeton, NJ: Princeton University Press, 2007.

10 Lila Abu-Lughod, 'Writing against Culture', in *Recapturing Anthropology: Working in the Present*, ed. Richard G. Fox. Santa Fe, NM: University of Washington Press, 1991: 158. The full quote – one of my current favourites – goes as follows: 'The particulars suggest that others live as we perceive ourselves living, not as robots programmed with "cultural" rules, but as people going through life agonizing over decisions, making mistakes, trying to make themselves look good, enduring tragedies and personal losses, enjoying others, and finding moments of happiness.'

11 The asymmetry between majority and minority mirrors what is commonly said about gender and ethnicity: it is women who are seen as defined by their gender, not men, and those from minority ethnic groups who are perceived as having an 'ethnicity', while the ethnic identity of the majority remains an unnoticed norm. See Nirmal Puwar, *Space Invaders: Race, Gender and Bodies Out of Place*. Oxford: Berg, 2004, for a good discussion of this.

12 Chandran Kukathas, 'Is Feminism Bad for Multiculturalism?' *Public Affairs Quarterly*, 15/2 (2001): 83–98.

13 Anne Phillips, *The Politics of Presence: The Political Representation of Gender, Ethnicity and Race*. Oxford and New York: Oxford University Press, 1995.

14 James Tully, *Strange Multiplicity: Constitutionalism in an Age of Diversity*. Cambridge: Cambridge University Press, 1995: 10.

15 The distinction between culture and cultural community is particularly clear in Will Kymlicka, *Liberalism, Community, and Culture*. Oxford: Clarendon Press, 1989: ch. 8.

16 For her response to some of the criticisms, see Susan Moller Okin, 'Multiculturalism and Feminism: No Simple Question, No Simple Answers', in *Minorities within Minorities: Equality, Rights and Diversity*, ed. Avigail Eisenberg and Jeff Spinner-Halev. Cambridge: Cambridge University Press, 2005: 67–89.
17 Will Kymlicka, 'Multicultural Citizenship: Practices, Policies and Theories', Auguste Comte Annual Lecture, London School of Economics, May 2008. See also Andrew Mason, 'Multiculturalism and the Critique of Essentialism', in *Multiculturalism and Political Theory*, ed. Anthony Simon Laden and David Owen. Cambridge and New York: Cambridge University Press, 2007: 221–43, for an argument that the main theories of multiculturalism do not depend on a flawed essentialism, or could relatively easily reconstruct their arguments to avoid it.
18 Bhikhu Parekh, *Rethinking Multiculturalism: Cultural Diversity and Political Theory*. Basingstoke: Macmillan, 2000: 241.
19 Gerd Baumann, *Contesting Culture: Discourses of Identity in Multi-Ethnic London*. Cambridge and New York: Cambridge University Press, 1996: 1.
20 Tariq Modood, *Multiculturalism: A Civic Idea*. Cambridge, UK, and Malden, MA: Polity, 2007.
21 Tariq Modood, 'Multiculturalism and Groups', *Social & Legal Studies*, 17/4 (2008): 550.
22 Rainer Baubock, 'Beyond Culturalism and Statism: Liberal Responses to Diversity', Working paper 6, *Eurosphere Working Paper Series*, 2008: 14.
23 Avishai Margalit and Joseph Raz, 'National Self-Determination', *The Journal of Philosophy*. 87/9 (1990): 439–61.
24 Modood, 'Multiculturalism and Groups': 550.
25 Phillips, *The Politics of Presence*.
26 Amartya Sen, *Commodities and Capabilities*. Amsterdam: North-Holland, 1985.

2 MULTICULTURALISM, UNIVERSALISM AND THE CLAIMS OF DEMOCRACY

1 Seyla Benhabib, '"Nous" et "les Autres": The Politics of Complex Cultural Dialogue in a Global Civilization', in *Multicultural Questions*, ed. Christian Joppke and Steven Lukes. Oxford: Oxford University Press, 1999: 44–64.
2 Carole Pateman, *The Sexual Contract*. Cambridge: Polity Press, 1988.
3 Iris Marion Young, *Justice and The Politics of Difference*. Princeton, NJ: Princeton University Press, 1990.
4 Carol Gilligan, *In a Different Voice: Psychological Theory and Women's Development*. Cambridge, MA: Harvard University Press, 1982; Seyla Benhabib, 'The Generalized and Concrete Other: The Kohlberg–

Gilligan Controversy and Feminist Theory', in *Feminism as Critique: Essays on the Politics of Gender in Late Capitalist Societies*, ed. Seyla Benhabib and Drucilla Cornell. Cambridge: Polity Press, 1987: 77–95.

5 Will Kymlicka, *Multicultural Citizenship: A Liberal Theory of Minority Rights*. Oxford: Oxford University Press, 1995.

6 Though I do not address it here, I find the distinction between voluntary and involuntary incorporation far from convincing. In its suggestion that migrants cannot later complain about the laws and practices of their 'chosen' country, it edges too close to John Locke's infamous argument about citizens demonstrating their 'consent' to the laws of their country whenever they enjoy the security that is provided by those laws.

7 Shachar, *Multicultural Jurisdictions*.

8 Kymlicka, *Multicultural Citizenship*: 169.

9 Kymlicka, *Multicultural Citizenship*: 170.

10 Her extended discussion of this is published as 'Feminism and Multiculturalism: Some Tensions'. An abbreviated version, with a number of critical and supportive responses, was published as Okin with respondents, *Is Multiculturalism Bad For Women?*

11 Okin, *Is Multiculturalism Bad for Women?*: 10.

12 Sawitri Saharso, 'Female Autonomy and Cultural Imperative: Two Hearts Beating Together', in *Citizenship in Diverse Societies*, ed. Will Kymlicka and Wayne Norman. Oxford: Oxford University Press, 2000: 224–44, argues for a modified understanding of autonomy that is worthy in Western liberal eyes but also compatible with what she sees as a different kind of autonomy, characteristic of Asian cultures. Parekh, *Rethinking Multiculturalism*, makes a stronger claim, arguing that, when liberals set up autonomy as the central moral norm, they deny the authentic otherness of non-liberal cultures. See also his 'A Varied Moral World', in Okin with respondents, *Is Multiculturalism Bad For Women?*: 69–75.

13 Martha Nussbaum, *Women and Human Development: The Capabilities Approach*. Cambridge and New York: Cambridge University Press, 2000.

14 Martha Nussbaum makes this point strongly in *Sex and Social Justice*. Oxford and New York: Oxford University Press, 1999.

15 Richard Bellamy, *Liberalism and Pluralism: Towards a Politics of Compromise*. New York: Routledge, 1999: 3.

16 Nussbaum, *Sex and Social Justice*: 32.

17 Phillips, *The Politics of Presence*.

18 In her discussion of these matters, Martha Nussbaum defends a political liberalism that respects different religious conceptions, even when these entail metaphysical positions about the superiority of men over women, or individuals choosing to live non-autonomous lives. See 'A Plea for Difficulty', in Okin with respondents, *Is Multiculturalism Bad For Women?*: 105–14.

3 DILEMMAS OF GENDER AND CULTURE: THE JUDGE,
   THE DEMOCRAT AND THE POLITICAL ACTIVIST

1 Shachar, *Multicultural Jurisdictions*: 4–17.
2 Susan Moller Okin, 'Mistresses of Their Own Destiny: Group Rights, Gender, and Realistic Rights of Exit', *Ethics*, 112/2 (2002): 205–30.
3 For example in Brian Barry, *Culture and Equality: An Egalitarian Critique of Multiculturalism*. Cambridge: Polity Press, 2001.
4 For example Benhabib, *The Claims of Culture*; Monique Deveaux, *Cultural Pluralism and Dilemmas of Justice*. Ithaca and London: Cornell University Press, 2000; Deveaux, *Gender and Justice in Multicultural Liberal States*; and Susan Song, *Justice, Gender, and the Politics of Multiculturalism*.
5 Parekh, *Rethinking Multiculturalism*.
6 Phillips and Saharso (eds.), 'The Rights of Women'.
7 Jacob Levy, *The Multiculturalism of Fear*. Oxford: Oxford University Press, 2000.
8 Brian Barry, 'The Muddles of Multiculturalism', *New Left Review*, 8 (2001): 49–71, 56.
9 In Monique Deveaux, 'Conflicting Equalities? Cultural Group Rights and Sex Equality', *Political Studies*, 48/3 (2000): 522–39. In her later work, Deveaux herself challenges assumptions of deep value diversity. See Deveaux, *Gender and Justice in Multicultural Liberal States*.
10 Narayan, 'Essence of Culture and a Sense of History'; Uma Narayan, 'Undoing the "Package Picture" of Cultures', *Signs*, 25/4 (2000): 1083–6.
11 I take this point from the work of Leti Volpp, who has carried out comparisons of legal cases in America involving under-age sex or marriage. She shows that these are treated as a problem of 'culture' when the individuals involved are immigrants of colour, but are rarely regarded as a reflection of American cultural values when the people involved are white. As she puts it, 'Behavior that causes discomfort – that we consider "bad" – is conceptualized only as culturally canonical for cultures assumed to lag behind the United States' (in 'Blaming Culture for Bad Behaviour', *Yale Journal of Law and the Humanities*, 12 (2000): 89–116).
12 Deveaux, 'Conflicting Equalities'.
13 The Supreme Court of India, *Writ petition (civil) No. 868/1986, Danial Latifi and Anr v. Union of India, 2001*. The Muslim Women's Act provides for 'a reasonable and fair provision' for maintenance during the *iddat* period – the three months or so before a divorced woman is able to remarry. The court ruled that this included provision in advance for future needs, not just her needs during that period.
14 Rajeswari Sunder Rajan, *The Scandal of the State: Women, Law and Citizenship in Postcolonial India*. Durham: Duke University Press, 2003: ch. 5.

15 For fuller discussion, see Anne Phillips and Moira Dustin, 'UK Initiatives on Forced Marriage: Regulation, Exit and Dialogue', *Political Studies*, 52/3 (2004): 531–51; Dustin and Phillips, 'Whose Agenda Is It?'

16 Tariq Modood, Richard Berthoud, Jane Lakey et al., *Ethnic Minorities in Britain: Diversity and Disadvantage. Fourth National Survey of Ethnic Minorities*. London: Policy Studies Institute, 1997.

17 Yunas Samad and John Eade, *Community Perceptions of Forced Marriage*. London: Community Liaison Unit, Foreign and Commonwealth Office, 2002: 112.

4 WHAT IS 'CULTURE'?

1 Raymond Williams, *Culture and Society*. London: Chatto and Windus, 1958.

2 Etienne Balibar, 'Is There a "Neo-Racism"?' in *Race, Nation, Class: Ambiguous Identities*, ed. Etienne Balibar and Immanuel Wallerstein. London: Verso, 1991: 17–28, 21.

3 For example, Terence Turner, 'Anthropology and Multiculturalism: What is Anthropology that Multiculturalists Should be Mindful of It?' in *Multiculturalism: A Critical Reader*, ed. David Theo Goldberg. Cambridge, MA, and Oxford: Blackwell, 1994: 406–25; Benhabib, *The Claims of Culture*; David Scott, 'Culture in Political Theory', *Political Theory*, 31/1 (2003): 92–115.

4 Kymlicka, *Multicultural Citizenship*: 1.

5 Kymlicka, *Multicultural Citizenship*: 18.

6 Shachar, *Multicultural Jurisdictions*: 2n. Later in the same paragraph, she even writes in the experience of oppression as one element in the definition: the groups share 'a unique history and collective memory, a distinct culture, a set of social norms, customs and traditions, or perhaps an experience of maltreatment by mainstream society or oppression by the state'.

7 Charles Taylor, 'The Politics of Recognition', in *Multiculturalism and the Politics of Recognition*, ed. Amy Gutmann. Princeton, NJ: Princeton University Press, 1992: 25–74, 38.

8 Levy, *The Multiculturalism of Fear*: 6.

9 See especially Uma Narayan's work: *Dislocating Cultures*; 'Essence of Culture'; and 'Undoing the "Package Picture" of Cultures'.

10 There are parallels in relation to national identity: the English, for example, are the hegemonic nationality within Great Britain, but have a less developed sense of what constitutes their national identity than the Welsh or the Scots.

11 Narayan, *Dislocating Cultures*: 105–17.

12 Alison Renteln, *The Cultural Defense*. New York and Oxford: Oxford University Press, 2004: 186–7.

13 Isabelle R. Gunning, 'Arrogant Perception, World Travelling and Multicultural Feminism: The Case of Female Genital Surgeries', *Columbia Human Rights Law Review*, 23 (1991–2): 189–248, 213.

14 For a fascinating dissection of the continuity argument, see Carolyn Pedwell, *Feminism, Culture and Embodied Practice: The Rhetorics of Comparison*. London and New York: Routledge.

15 Volpp, 'Feminism and Multiculturalism': 1181.

16 Volpp, 'Blaming Culture for Bad Behaviour'.

17 Tostan, *Breakthrough in Senegal: The Process that Ended Female Genital Cutting in 31 Villages*. Washinton, DC: US Agency for International Development, 1999.

18 E.g. in Dara Carr, *Female Genital Surgery: Findings from the Demographic and Health Surveys Program*. Calverton, MD: Macro International Inc., 1997.

19 Gerry Mackie, 'Female Genital Cutting: The Beginning of the End', in *Female 'Circumcision' in Africa: Culture, Controversy and Change*, ed. Bettina Shell-Duncan and Ylva Hernlund. Boulder, CO, and London: Lynne Rienner Publishers, 2000: 253–82.

20 This is the presumption in Gerry Mackie's account which draws on the more universalistic explanations of human conduct found in game theory. I may have been over-influenced by his account.

21 Adam Kuper, *Culture: The Anthropologists' Account*. Cambridge, MA, and London: Harvard University Press, 1999: 10.

22 Saba Mahmood, *Politics of Piety: The Islamic Revival and the Feminist Subject*. Princeton, NJ: Princeton University Press, 2005: 14. For a related argument in the context of eighteenth-century Quaker women, see Phyllis Mack, 'Religion, Feminism and the Problem of Agency: Reflections on Eighteenth-Century Quakerism', *Signs*, 29/1 (2003): 149–77.

5 WHAT'S WRONG WITH ESSENTIALISM?

1 Barbara Arneil, Monique Deveaux, Rita Dhamoon and Avigail Eisenberg (eds.), *Sexual Justice / Cultural Justice: Critical Perspectives in Political Theory*. New York and London: Routledge, 2006.

2 Shachar, 'Feminism and Multiculturalism'.

3 Ian Hacking, *The Social Construction of What?* Cambridge, MA, and London: Harvard University Press, 1999: 17.

4 Diana Fuss, *Essentially Speaking*. New York: Routledge, 1989.

5 Gayatri Chakravorty Spivak, 'Subaltern Studies: Deconstructing Historiography', in *In Other Worlds: Essays in Cultural Politics*, ed. Ranajit Guha and Gayatri Chakravorty Spivak. Oxford: Oxford University Press, 1988: 197–221, 205.

6   Gerd Baumann, *Contesting Culture: Discourses of Identity in Multi-Ethnic London.* Cambridge and New York: Cambridge University Press, 1996: 1.

7   This may expose Baumann to Bruno Latour's complaint against the archetypical 'critical sociologist', who, when asked whether constructed reality is constructed or real, blandly responds that it is both. Latour presents this as the ultimate trivialization. He rejects both the idea that we could conjure something into existence purely through our categories, and that we could then find ourselves fooled by them. ' "We" never build a world of our own delusion because there exists no such free creator as "us" . . . "we" are never deluded by a world of fancy because there exists no force strong enough to transform us into the mere slaves of powerful illusion' (Bruno Latour, 'The Promises of Constructivism', in *Chasing Technoscience: Matrix of Materiality*, eds. Don Idhe and Evan Selinger. Bloomington, IN: Indiana University Press, 2003: 27–46).

8   Lawrence Hirschfeld, *Race in the Making: Cognition, Culture, and the Child's Construction of Human Kinds.* Cambridge, MA, and London: MIT Press, 1996. See also the discussion in Ann Laura Stoler, 'On Political and Psychological Essentialisms', *Ethos*, 25/1 (1997): 101–6.

9   Hirschfeld, *Race in the Making*: 196.

10 Rogers Brubaker, 'Ethnicity without Groups', *European Journal of Sociology*, 43/3 (2002): 163–89.

11 Brubaker, 'Ethnicity without Groups': 167.

12 Janet Shibley Hyde, 'The Gender Similarities Hypothesis', *American Psychologist*, 60/6 (2005): 581–92. A meta-analysis is an aggregation of existing research findings from what might be hundreds of similar studies on a particular question, so her study is a 'meta-'meta-analysis.

13 Iris Marion Young, *On Female Body Experience: 'Throwing Like a Girl' and Other Essays.* Oxford: Oxford University Press, 2005.

14 Hacking, *The Social Construction of What?*

15 Kasper Lippert-Rasmussen, 'Racial Profiling versus Community', *Journal of Applied Philosophy*, 23/2 (2006): 191–205. Lippert-Rasmussen makes these observations in the context of a powerful argument *against* racial profiling.

16 Narayan, 'Essence of Culture and a Sense of History'.

17 Brubaker, 'Ethnicity without Groups': 164.

18 Butler, *Gender Trouble.*

19 Modood, *Multiculturalism: A Civic Idea*: 93.

20 Susan Moller Okin, *Justice, Gender and the Family.* New York: Basic Books, 1989: 171.

21 Joan Scott, *Only Paradoxes to Offer: French Feminists and the Rights of Man.* Cambridge, MA: Harvard University Press, 1996: 3–4.

22 Narayan, 'Essence of Culture and a Sense of History': 86.

23 Spivak, 'Subaltern Studies: Deconstructing Historiography': 205.

24 Iris Marion Young, 'Gender as Seriality: Thinking about Women as a Social Collective', *Signs*, 19/3 (1994): 713–38, 728.

6 WHEN CULTURE MEANS GENDER: ISSUES OF CULTURAL
    DEFENCE IN THE ENGLISH COURTS

1   Key articles include Julia P. Sams, 'The Availability of the "Cultural Defense" as an Excuse for Criminal Behavior', *Georgia Journal of International and Comparative Law*, 16 (1986): 335–54; Paul J. Magnarella, 'Justice in a Culturally Pluralistic Society: The Culture Defense on Trial', *The Journal of Ethnic Studies*, 19 (1991): 65–84; Alison Dundes Renteln, 'A Justification of the Cultural Defense as a Partial Excuse', *California Review of Law and Women's Studies*, 2 (1993): 437–526; Daina C. Chiu, 'The Cultural Defense: Beyond Exclusion, Assimilation, and Guilty Liberalism', *California Law Review*, 82 (1994): 1053–1128; Leti Volpp, '(Mis)identifying Culture: Asian Women and the "Cultural Defense" ', *Harvard Women's Law Journal*, 17 (1994): 57–101; Doriane Lambelet Coleman, 'Individualizing Justice through Multiculturalism: The Liberal's Dilemma', *Columbia Law Review*, 95 (1996): 1093–166; Nancy S. Kim, 'The Cultural Defence and the Problems of Cultural Preemption: A Framework for Analysis', *New Mexico Law Review*, 27 (1997): 101–39; Jeroen Van Broeck, 'Cultural Defence and Culturally Motivated Crimes', *European Journal of Crime, Criminal Law and Criminal Justice*, 9/1 (2001): 1–31.
2   The issues associated with cultural defence feature in Susan Moller Okin's highly influential essay *Is Multiculturalism Bad for Women?*, alongside a range of other illustrations designed to highlight tensions between feminism and multiculturalism.
3   *People* v. *Chen* No 87-7774 (Supreme Court, NY County, 2 December 1988).
4   For good discussions of this case, see Volpp, '(Mis)identifying Culture'. In Volpp's assessment, the witness was testifying more to 'his own *American* fantasy' of Chinese life: divorce rates have in fact been rising sharply in China, where less than 12 per cent of the population now think of divorce as disgraceful; and the expert witness admitted that he couldn't actually recall a single instance of a man killing his adulterous wife.
5   Cited in Kim, 'The Cultural Defence': 120.
6   *People of the State of California* v. *Kong Pheng Moua* No. 315972 (Fresno County Superior Court, 7 February 1985).
7   Volpp, '(Mis)identifying Culture': 77.
8   Coleman, 'Individualizing Justice through Multiculturalism': 1159.
9   Magnarella, 'Justice in a Culturally Pluralistic Society': 67.
10 Van Broeck, 'Cultural Defence and Culturally Motivated Crimes': 5.
11 Unreported, but noted in [1975] 24 ICLQ 136.

12 In his sympathetic assessment of the case for ending the legal prohibi-
    tion on the use of cannabis by Rastafarians, even Sebastian Poulter
    inclined to the view that the prohibition should be ended for everyone,
    rather than just for those who can establish some legitimate cultural or
    religious claim. Note also that the argument in this case turns on reli-
    gion rather than a more generalized notion of culture (Poulter, *Ethni-
    city, Law and Human Rights: The English Experience*. Oxford:
    Clarendon Press, 1998: ch. 9.

13 Okin, 'Feminism and Multiculturalism: Some Tensions': 667.

14 *R* v. *Bailey* [1964] CLR 671; *R* v. *Byefield* [1967] CLR 378.

15 For example, *R* v. *Shabir Hussain*, Newcastle Crown Court, 28 July
    1998 (transcript: J. L. Harpham Ltd); *R* v. *Shazad, Shakeela and Iftikhar
    Naz*, Nottingham High Court, 24–25 May 1999 (transcript: Cater
    Walsh and Co.); *R* v. *Faqir Mohammed*, Manchester Crown Court, 18
    Feb. 2002 (transcript: Cater Walsh and Co.).

16 *People* v. *Kimura* No. A-091133 (Super Ct, LA County, 24 April 1985).

17 Sams, 'The Availability of the "Cultural Defense" as an Excuse for
    Criminal Behavior': 343.

18 Okin, *Is Multiculturalism Bad For Women?*: 19.

19 Pascale Fournier, 'The Ghettoization of Difference in Canada: "Rape
    by Culture" or the Danger of a Cultural Defence in Criminal Law
    Trials', *The Manitoba Law Journal*, 29/81 (2002): 81–113, 88.

20 Fournier, 'The Ghettoisation of Differences in Canada': 93.

21 The case is discussed at length in Fournier, as is a parallel case where
    a Muslim man was found guilty of sexual misbehaviour – including
    anal intercourse – with his wife's daughter, but was treated with leni-
    ency, partly, it seems, because he had respected the value Islam attaches
    to virginity, and had 'spared his victim' from vaginal intercourse. In
    this case, the sentence was raised on appeal.

22 Coleman, for example, has been said to replicate a colonialist feminism
    that attaches all the virtues of gender equality to the West and all the
    vices of patriarchy to the Rest; she seems to take it as given that non-
    European migrant cultures really are defined by patterns of sexual and
    parental violence; and it is because she buys into these stereotypical
    representations of non-European cultures that she is so opposed to the
    use of cultural defence. Volpp, 'Talking "Culture" '.

23 Volpp, 'Blaming Culture for Bad Behaviour': 89, 96. In one of the cases
    she discusses, Texan police and child welfare officials launched a
    massive search for a pregnant runaway – believed at that point to be
    only 10 years old – and her boyfriend; when the couple were located,
    the girl was placed in a foster home and her 22-year-old boyfriend in
    a maximum security facility, charged with aggravated sexual assault of
    a child. Charges were dropped when it emerged that the girl, Adela
    Quintana, was in fact fourteen (above the age of consent to sexual
    intercourse in Texan law), and a family court judge ruled that the
    couple had a valid common-law marriage. In this case, both parties

were of Mexican origin, and the events were widely discussed in the press as an illustration of the collision of cultures. It was assumed in these discussions, and indeed argued in the courts, that marriage between an adolescent girl and an older man was a reflection of 'Mexican culture'. In a similar case in Maryland, where Tina Compton, a 13-year-old (white) girl married a 29-year-old (white) man, none of the media debate and public outcry made any reference to the marriage as a cultural phenomenon. It seems that it is only when the parties concerned are relatively recent migrants from non-European countries that child marriage becomes a reflection of cultural traditions.

24 Cited in Chiu, 'The Cultural Defense': 1053.
25 Volpp, 'Talking "Culture" ': 1612.
26 Volpp '(Mis)identifying Culture': 57.
27 *Equal Treatment Bench Book*, London: Judicial Studies Board, 2008, available at http://www.jsboard.co.uk/etac/etbb/index.htm: chs. 1.1, 1.2.
28 Barry, *Culture and Equality*: 34.
29 The most comprehensive early review is Sebastian Poulter, *English Law and Ethnic Minority Customs*. London: Butterworths, 1986.
30 It is hard to see how this last can be effective, short of intrusive examination of young girls by immigration officers on their return to the UK. For more detailed discussion of this and other UK policy initiatives, see Dustin and Phillips, 'Whose Agenda Is It?'
31 *Alhaji Mohamed* v. *Knott* [1969] 1 QB 1.
32 Alex Samuels, 'Legal Recognition and Protection of Minority Customs in a Plural Society in England', *Anglo-American Law Review*, 10/4 (1981): 241–56.
33 HC 3069 of 85–6; see Poulter, *Ethnicity, Law and Human Rights*: 53.
34 A marriage is potentially polygamous if it was conducted under a jurisdiction that allows the man to take more than one wife; even if he intends to remain monogamous, the marriage is deemed void within the UK.
35 Combined with Immigration Rules HC555 of 1988.
36 Under the Social Security and Family Allowances (Polygamous Marriage) Regulations 1975, SI 1975/561, a widow of a potentially polygamous marriage (i.e. one contracted under a jurisdiction that allows polygamy) which was de facto monogamous is entitled to the same widow's pension as a widow of a monogamous marriage; she will not, however, get the pension if there is a second wife living elsewhere (*Bibi* v. *Chief Adjudication Officer* (Court of Appeal Civil Division) 1998).
37 National Health Service (Superannuation) (Amendment) Regulation 1989, SI 1989/804.
38 Alex Samuels argues that 'If a person is bona fide polygamous then . . . he ought to be allowed to take a polygamous wife in England provided that he conform to the law of the polygamous group to which he belongs, or abroad, provided that he conforms to the local law. There

is no longer any reason, if ever there was, for making English law the personal law of all persons domiciled in England. A personal law based upon personal religion or culture is far more acceptable in a multi-racial society' (Samuels, 'Legal Recognition and Protection of Minority Customs': 251).

39   E.g. in Aileen McColgan, 'In Defence of Battered Women Who Kill', *Oxford Journal of Legal Studies*, 13/4 (1993): 508–29; Fiona Railt and Suzanne Zeedyk, *The Implicit Relation of Psychology and Law: Women and Syndrome Evidence*. Philadelphia and London: Routledge, 2000; Alan Norrie, *Crime, Reason and History: A Critical Introduction to Criminal Law*. London: Weidenfeld & Nicolson, 2001.

40   Aileen McColgan, 'General Defences', in *Feminist Perspectives on Criminal Law*, ed. Donald Nicolson and Lois Bibbings. London: Routledge, 2000: 137–58, 151.

41   McColgan suggests that 'the most interesting issue about general defences is the non-availability of a defence related to fear or despair, save to the extent that this can be brought within the reasonableness requirement of justifiable force' ('General Defences': 155).

42   *R* v. *Bailey* [1964] CLR 671; *R* v. *Byfield* [1967] CLR 378.

43   Sebastian Poulter, 'The Significance of Ethnic Minority Customs and Traditions in English Criminal Law', *New Community*, 16/1 (1989): 121–8, 122.

44   *R* v. *Bibi* [1980] 1 WLR 1193.

45   *R* v. *Kiranjit Ahluwalia*, unreported case, Lewes Crown Court, 6 and 7 December 1989 (transcript: Hibbit and Sanders).

46   *R* v. *Ahluwalia* [1992] 4 All ER 889.

47   Drawing on the appeal case rather than the initial trial, Matthew Rowlinson stresses the way Ahluwalia's intentionality was effaced: 'Re-Reading Criminal Law: Gendering the Mental Element', in *Feminist Perspectives on Criminal Law*, ed. Donald Nicolson and Lois Bibbings. London: Routledge, 2000: 101–22, 114–16.

48   *R* v. *Zoora Ghulam Shah*, Court of Appeal, Criminal Division, 30 April 1998 (transcript: Smith Bernal).

49   *R* v. *Shazad, Shakeela and Iftikhar Naz*, Nottingham High Court, May 1999 (transcript: Cater Walsh and Co.). See also Hannana Siddiqui, 'The Ties That Bind', *Index on Censorship*, 29/1 (2000): 50–3.

50   *R* v. *Shakeela Naz*, 2000 ECWA Crim 24.

51   *R* v. *Faqir Mohammed*, Manchester Crown Court, 18 Feb. 2002 (transcript: Cater Walsh and Co.).

52   *R* v. *Shabir Hussain* [1997] EWCA Crim 2876.

53   *R* v. *Shabir Hussain*, Newcastle Crown Court, 28 July 1998 (transcript: J. L. Harpham Ltd).

54   Cited in Chiu, 'The Cultural Defense': 1118–19.

55   *People* v. *Chen* (Supreme Court, NY County, 2 December 1988).

56   *People of the State of California* v. *Kong Pheng Moua* (Fresno County Superior Court, 7 February 1985).

57   Chiu, 'The Cultural Defense': 1113–20.
58   E.g., Donald Nicolson and Lois Bibbings (eds.), *Feminist Perspectives on Criminal Law*. London: Routledge, 2000.
59   Chiu, 'The Cultural Defense': 1114.

7   FREE TO DECIDE FOR ONESELF

1   Alison Jaggar, *Feminist Politics and Human Nature*. Totowa, NJ: Rowman and Littlefield, 1983; Jennifer Nedelsky, 'Reconceiving Autonomy: Sources, Thoughts and Possibilities', *Yale Journal of Law and Feminism*, 1/1 (1989): 7–36; Catriona MacKenzie and Natalie Stoljar (eds.), *Relational Autonomy: Feminist Perspectives on Autonomy, Agency and the Social Self*. New York and Oxford: Oxford University Press, 2000; Marilyn Friedman, *Autonomy, Gender, Politics*. Oxford: Oxford University Press, 2003.
2   For example Martha Nussbaum, 'The Feminist Critique of Liberalism', in *Sex and Social Justice*. New York and Oxford: Oxford University Press, 1999: 55–80.
3   Simone de Beauvoir, *The Second Sex*. London: New English Library, 1969: 338. (First published in France in 1949; first English translation, 1953.)
4   Nussbaum, *Women and Human Development*: esp. ch. 2.
5   Jon Elster, *Sour Grapes: Studies in the Subversion of Rationality*. Cambridge: Cambridge University Press, 1983; Cass Sunstein, 'Preferences and Politics', *Philosophy and Public Affairs*, 20 (1991): 3–34; Amartya Sen, 'Gender Inequality and Theories of Justice', in *Women, Culture and Development: A Study of Human Capabilities*, ed. Martha Nussbaum and Jonathan Glover. Oxford: Clarendon Press, 1995: 259–73.
6   I take this to be the position adopted by Chandran Kukathas, *The Liberal Archipelago: A Theory of Diversity and Freedom*. Oxford: Oxford University Press, 2003. Kukathas argues that what matters is not so much whether decisions are voluntary (in the Nussbaum sense of informed and reflective acceptance), as that they should not be forced.
7   Pateman, *The Sexual Contract*: 7–8 (my italics).
8   Samad and Eade, *Community Perceptions of Forced Marriage*.
9   Nazia Khanum, *Forced Marriage, Family Cohesion and Community Engagement: National Learning through a Case Study of Luton*, 2008. www.luton.gov.uk/Media%20Library/Pdf/Chief%20executives/ Equalities/Forced%20Marriage%20Report%20-%20Final%20 Version.pdf.
10   Kalwant Bhopal, 'South Asian Women and Arranged Marriages in East London', in *Ethnicity, Gender and Social Change*, ed. Rohit Barot, Harriet Bradley and Steve Fenton. Basingstoke: Macmillan and New York: St Martin's Press, 1999: 117–34, 21.

11   Home Office, *A Choice by Right – The Report of the Working Group on Forced Marriage*. London: Home Office Communications Directorate, 2000: 10.
12   Modood, Berthoud, Lakey et al., *Ethnic Minorities in Britain*: 318.
13   Kukathas, *The Liberal Archipelago*: 107.
14   Sawitri Saharso, 'Feminist Ethics, Autonomy and the Politics of Multiculturalism', *Feminist Theory*, 4/2 (2003): 199–215.
15   Karl Marx, *Capital Volume I*. London and New York: Penguin, 1976: 280.
16   Pateman, *The Sexual Contract*: 153.
17   Sibyl Schwarzenbach, 'Contractarians and Feminists Debate Prostitution', *Review of Law and Social Change*, 18 (1990–1): 103–30; Wendy Brown, 'Liberalism's Family Values', in *States of Injury: Power and Freedom in Late Modernity*. Princeton, NJ: Princeton University Press, 1995: 135–65; Moira Gatens, *Imaginary Bodies: Ethics, Power and Corporeality*. London and New York: Routledge, 1996; Nancy Fraser, 'Beyond the Master/Subject Model: On Carole Pateman's *The Sexual Contract*', in *Justice Interruptus: Critical Reflections on the 'Postsocialist' Condition*. London and New York: Routledge, 1997: 225–36; Cecile Fabre, *Whose Body Is It Anyway? Justice and the Integrity of the Person*. Oxford: Clarendon Press, 2006.
18   Martha C. Nussbaum, ' "Whether from Reason or Prejudice": Taking Money for Bodily Services', in *Sex and Social Justice*: 276–98.
19   Pateman, *The Sexual Contract*: 216.
20   Carole Pateman, 'Self-ownership and Property in the Person', *Journal of Political Philosophy*, 10/1 (2002): 20–53, 33.
21   Pateman, *The Sexual Contract*: 232.

8   CONSENT, AUTONOMY AND COERCION:
FORCED MARRIAGE, PUBLIC POLICY AND THE COURTS

1   For more detail on the evolution of UK policy, see Phillips and Dustin, 'UK Initiatives on Forced Marriage; and Dustin and Phillips, 'Whose Agenda Is It?' See also Southall Black Sisters, *Forced Marriage: An Abuse of Human Rights. One Year After 'A Choice by Right'*. London: Southall Black Sisters, 2001; Monique Deveaux, 'Personal Autonomy and Cultural Tradition. The Arranged Marriage Debate in Britain', in *Sexual Justice / Cultural Justice*, ed. Barbara Arneil, Monique Deveaux, Rita Dhamoon and Avigail Eisenberg. New York and London: Routledge, 2006: 139–66.
2   Wilson, 'The Forced Marriage Debate and the British State'.
3   Home Office, *A Choice by Right*.
4   Home Office, *Forced Marriage: A Wrong Not a Right*. London: Foreign & Commonwealth Office, 2005.
5   Home Office, *A Choice by Right*: 10.

6 *NS* v. *MI* [2006] EWHC 1646 (Fam), paras. 2–4.
7 *R* v. *Ghulam Rasool* [1990–1] 12 Cr. App. R (S.) 771.
8 The other route has been non-consummation of the marriage. But petitioners then have to establish their physical or emotional incapacity –
   either a medical incapacity or an 'invincible repugnance' – and are
   unlikely to win the case if they are felt only to be unwilling to have sex
   with their spouse. Alternatively, a petitioner may win a grant of nullity
   on the grounds of the other party's 'wilful refusal to consummate'.
   Marrying and then changing your mind is seen as a matter for the
   divorce courts, not for nullity proceedings.
9 *Singh* v. *Singh* [1971] 2 All ER 828.
10 *Hirani* v. *Hirani* [1983] 4 FLR 232.
11 *P* v. *R (Forced Marriage: Annulment: Procedure)* [2003] 1 FLR 661,
   paras. 17–18; *NS* v. *MI* [2006] EWHC 1646 (Fam), paras. 10–11. The
   cheaper remedy is divorce, but, as both judges argue, divorce is not the
   appropriate remedy for a forced marriage, because it leaves the petitioner with the stigma of divorce.
12 *Mahmood* v. *Mahmood* [1993] SLT 589.
13 *Mahmud* v. *Mahmud* [1994] SLT 599.
14 *Re KR (A Child) (Abduction: Forcible Removal by Parents)* [1999] 2
   FLR 542. The judge in the case authorized the publication of his judgment (not the norm in family law cases) so as to guide future
   practice.
15 *Re M Minors (Repatriated Orphans)* [2003] EWHC 852.
16 *Re SK (An Adult) (Forced Marriage: Appropriate Relief)* [2004] EWHC
   3202 (Fam), para. 15.
17 *In the Matter of SA* [2005] EWHC 2942 (Fam).
18 *In the Matter of SA*, para. 78.
19 *Re K; A local authority* v. *N and others* [2005] EWHC 2956 (Fam),
   para. 93.
20 *Singh* v. *Bhakar* [2006] Fam Law 637.
21 To be more precise, they can marry – like anyone – at the standard
   legal age, but cannot apply to bring their new spouses to live with them
   in the UK.
22 Wilson, 'The Forced Marriage Debate': 27.

Bibliography

Abu-Lughod, Lila. 'Writing against Culture', in *Recapturing Anthropology: Working in the Present*, ed. Richard G. Fox. Santa Fe, NM: University of Washington Press, 1991: 137–62.

Arneil, Barbara, Deveaux, Monique, Dhamoon, Rita and Eisenberg, Avigail (eds). *Sexual Justice / Cultural Justice: Critical Perspectives in Political Theory*. New York and London: Routledge, 2006.

Balibar, Etienne. 'Is There a "Neo-Racism"?' in *Race, Nation, Class: Ambiguous Identities*, ed. Etienne Balibar and Immanuel Wallerstein. London: Verso, 1991: 17–28.

Barry, Brian. *Culture and Equality: An Egalitarian Critique of Multiculturalism*. Cambridge: Polity Press, 2001.

'The Muddles of Multiculturalism', *New Left Review*, 8 (2001): 49–71.

Baubock, Rainer. 'Beyond Culturalism and Statism: Liberal Responses to Diversity', Working paper 6, *Eurosphere Working Paper Series*, 2008: 1–34.

Baumann, Gerd. *Contesting Culture: Discourses of Identity in Multi-Ethnic London*. Cambridge and New York: Cambridge University Press, 1996.

Beauvoir, Simone de. *The Second Sex*. London: New English Library, 1969. (First published in France in 1949; first English translation, 1953.)

Bellamy, Richard. *Liberalism and Pluralism: Towards a Politics of Compromise*. New York: Routledge, 1999.

Benhabib, Seyla. 'The Generalized and Concrete Other: The Kohlberg–Gilligan Controversy and Feminist Theory', in *Feminism as Critique: Essays on the Politics of Gender in Late Capitalist Societies*, ed. Seyla Benhabib and Drucilla Cornell. Cambridge: Polity Press, 1987: 77–95.

' "Nous" et "les Autres": The Politics of Complex Cultural Dialogue in a Global Civilization', in *Multicultural Questions*, ed. Christian Joppke and Steven Lukes. Oxford: Oxford University Press, 1999: 44–64.

The Claims of Culture: Equality and Diversity in the Global Era. Princeton, NJ, and Oxford: Princeton University Press, 2002.

Bhopal, Kalwant. 'South Asian Women and Arranged Marriages in East London', in *Ethnicity, Gender and Social Change*, ed. Rohit Barot, Harriet Bradley and Steve Fenton. London and Basingstoke: Macmillan and St Martin's Press, 1999: 117–34.

Brown, Wendy. 'Liberalism's Family Values', in *States of Injury: Power and Freedom in Late Modernity*. Princeton, NJ: Princeton University Press, 1995: 135–65.

Brubaker, Rogers. 'Ethnicity without Groups', *European Journal of Sociology*, 43/3 (2002): 163–89.

Butler, Judith. *Gender Trouble: Feminism and the Subversion of Identity*. New York and London: Routledge, 1990.

Carr, Dara. *Female Genital Surgery: Findings from the Demographic and Health Surveys Program*. Calverton, MD: Macro International Inc., 1997.

Chiu, Daina C. 'The Cultural Defense: Beyond Exclusion, Assimilation, and Guilty Liberalism', *California Law Review*, 82 (1994): 1053–128.

Coleman, Doriane Lambelet. 'Individualizing Justice through Multiculturalism: The Liberal's Dilemma', *Columbia Law Review*, 95 (1996): 1093–166.

Deveaux, Monique. 'Conflicting Equalities? Cultural Group Rights and Sex Equality', *Political Studies*, 48/3 (2000): 522–39.

Cultural Pluralism and Dilemmas of Justice. Ithaca and London: Cornell University Press, 2000.

'Personal Autonomy and Cultural Tradition. The Arranged Marriage Debate in Britain', in *Sexual Justice / Cultural Justice*, ed. Barbara Arneil, Monique Deveaux, Rita Dhamoon, and Avigail Eisenberg. New York and London: Routledge, 2006: 139–66.

Gender and Justice in Multicultural Liberal States. Oxford and New York: Oxford University Press, 2008.

Dustin, Moira and Phillips, Anne. 'Whose Agenda Is It? Abuses of Women and Abuses of "Culture" in Britain', *Ethnicities*, 8/3 (2008): 405–24.

Elster, Jon. *Sour Grapes: Studies in the Subversion of Rationality*. Cambridge: Cambridge University Press, 1983.

Equal Treatment Bench Book, London: Judicial Studies Board, 2008, available at www.jsboard.co.uk/etac/etbb/index.htm, last accessed 12 Dec. 2008.

Fabre, Cecile. *Whose Body Is It Anyway? Justice and the Integrity of the Person*. Oxford: Clarendon Press, 2006.

Fournier, Pascale. 'The Ghettoization of Difference in Canada: "Rape by Culture" or the Danger of a Cultural Defence in Criminal Law Trials', *The Manitoba Law Journal*, 29/81 (2002): 81–113.

Fraser, Nancy. 'Beyond the Master/Subject Model: On Carole Pateman's *The Sexual Contract*', in *Justice Interruptus: Critical Reflections on the 'Postsocialist' Condition*. London and New York: Routledge, 1997: 225–36.

Friedman, Marilyn. *Autonomy, Gender, Politics*. Oxford: Oxford University Press, 2003.

Fuss, Diana. *Essentially Speaking*. New York: Routledge, 1989.

Gatens, Moira. 'A Critique of the Sex/Gender Distinction', in *Beyond Marxism? Interventions after Marx*, ed. Judith Allen and Paul Patten. Sydney: Intervention Publications, 1983: 143–60.

Imaginary Bodies: Ethics, Power and Corporeality. London and New York: Routledge, 1996.

Gilligan, Carol. *In a Different Voice: Psychological Theory and Women's Development*. Cambridge, MA: Harvard University Press, 1982.

Gunning, Isabelle R. 'Arrogant Perception, World Travelling and Multicultural Feminism: The Case of Female Genital Surgeries', *Columbia Human Rights Law Review*, 23 (1991–2): 189–248.

Hacking, Ian. *The Social Construction of What?* Cambridge, MA, and London: Harvard University Press, 1999.

Hirschfeld, Lawrence. *Race in the Making: Cognition, Culture, and the Child's Construction of Human Kinds*. Cambridge, MA, and London: MIT Press, 1996.

Home Office. *A Choice by Right – The Report of the Working Group on Forced Marriage*. London: Home Office Communications Directorate, 2000.

Forced Marriage: A Wrong Not a Right, London: Foreign & Commonwealth Office, 2005.

Hyde, Janet Shibley. 'The Gender Similarities Hypothesis', *American Psychologist*, 60/6 (2005): 581–92.

Jaggar, Alison. *Feminist Politics and Human Nature*. Totowa, NJ: Rowman and Littlefield, 1983.

Khanum, Nazia. *Forced Marriage, Family Cohesion and Community Engagement: National Learning through a Case Study of Luton*, 2008, available at www.luton.gov.uk/Media%20Library/Pdf/Chief%20executives/Equalities/Forced%20Marriage%20Report%20-%20Final%20Version.pdf.

Kim, Nancy S. 'The Cultural Defence and the Problems of Cultural Preemption: A Framework for Analysis', *New Mexico Law Review*, 27 (1997): 101–39.

Kukathas, Chandran. 'Is Feminism Bad for Multiculturalism?' *Public Affairs Quarterly*, 15/2 (2001): 83–98.

The Liberal Archipelago: A Theory of Diversity and Freedom. Oxford: Oxford University Press, 2003.

Kuper, Adam. *Culture: The Anthropologists' Account*. Cambridge, MA, and London: Harvard University Press, 1999.

Kymlicka, Will. *Liberalism, Community, and Culture*. Oxford: Clarendon Press, 1989.

Multicultural Citizenship: A Liberal Theory of Minority Rights. Oxford: Oxford University Press, 1995.

Latour, Bruno. 'The Promises of Constructivism', in *Chasing Technoscience: Matrix of Materiality*, ed. Don Idhe and Evan Selinger. Bloomington, IN: Indiana University Press, 2003: 27–46.

Levy, Jacob T. *The Multiculturalism of Fear*. Oxford: Oxford University Press, 2000.

Lippert-Rasmussen, Kasper. 'Racial Profiling versus Community', *Journal of Applied Philosophy*, 23/2 (2006): 191–205.

Mack, Phyllis. 'Religion, Feminism and the Problem of Agency: Reflections on Eighteenth-Century Quakerism', *Signs*, 29/1 (2003): 149–77.

MacKenzie, Catriona and Stoljar, Natalie (eds.). *Relational Autonomy: Feminist Perspectives on Autonomy, Agency and the Social Self*. New York and Oxford: Oxford University Press, 2000.

Mackie, Gerry. 'Female Genital Cutting: The Beginning of the End', in *Female 'Circumcision' in Africa: Culture, Controversy and Change*, ed. Bettina Shell-Duncan and Ylva Hernlund. Boulder, CO, and London: Lynne Rienner Publishers, 2000: 253–82.

Magnarella, Paul J. 'Justice in a Culturally Pluralistic Society: The Culture Defense on Trial', *The Journal of Ethnic Studies*, 19 (1991): 65–84.

Mahmood, Saba. *Politics of Piety: The Islamic Revival and the Feminist Subject*. Princeton, NJ: Princeton University Press, 2005.

Margalit, Avishai and Raz, Joseph. 'National Self-Determination', *The Journal of Philosophy*, 87/9 (1990): 439–61.

Marx, Karl. *Capital Volume I*. London and New York: Penguin, 1976.

Mason, Andrew. 'Multiculturalism and the Critique of Essentialism', in *Multiculturalism and Political Theory*, ed. Anthony Simon Laden and David Owen. Cambridge and New York: Cambridge University Press, 2007: 221–43.

McColgan, Aileen. 'In Defence of Battered Women Who Kill', *Oxford Journal of Legal Studies*, 13/4 (1993): 508–29.
'General Defences', in *Feminist Perspectives on Criminal Law*, ed. Donald Nicolson and Lois Bibbings. London: Routledge, 2000: 137–58.

Modood, Tariq. *Multiculturalism: A Civic Idea*. Cambridge, and Malden, MA: Polity, 2007.
'Multiculturalism and Groups', *Social & Legal Studies*, 17/4 (2008): 549–53.

Modood, Tariq, Berthoud, Richard, Lakey, Jane, Nazroo, James, Smith, Patten, Virdee, Satnam and Beishon, Sharon. *Ethnic Minorities in Britain: Diversity and Disadvantage. Fourth National Survey of Ethnic Minorities*. London: Policy Studies Institute, 1997.

Narayan, Uma. *Dislocating Cultures: Identities, Traditions, and Third World Feminism*. London and New York: Routledge, 1997.
'Essence of Culture and a Sense of History: A Feminist Critique of Cultural Essentialism', *Hypatia*, 13/2 (1998): 86–106.
'Undoing the "Package Picture" of Cultures', *Signs*, 25/4 (2000): 1083–6.

Nedelsky, Jennifer. 'Reconceiving Autonomy: Sources, Thoughts and Possibilities', *Yale Journal of Law and Feminism*, 1/1 (1989): 7–36.

Nicolson, Donald and Bibbings, Lois (eds.). *Feminist Perspectives on Criminal Law*. London: Routledge, 2000.

Norrie, Alan. *Crime, Reason and History: A Critical Introduction to Criminal Law*. London: Weidenfeld & Nicolson, 2001.

Norton, Anne. 'Review Essay on Euben, Okin and Nussbaum', *Political Theory*, 29/5 (2001): 736–49.

Nussbaum, Martha. 'A Plea for Difficulty', in Susan Moller Okin with respondents, *Is Multiculturalism Bad for Women?* ed. Joshua Cohen, Matthew Howard and Martha C. Nussbaum. Princeton, NJ: Princeton University Press, 1999: 105–14.

Sex and Social Justice. Oxford and New York: Oxford University Press, 1999.

Women and Human Development: The Capabilities Approach. Cambridge and New York: Cambridge University Press, 2000.

Okin, Susan Moller. *Justice, Gender and the Family*. New York: Basic Books, 1989.

'Feminism and Multiculturalism: Some Tensions', *Ethics*, 108 (1998): 661–84.

'Mistresses of Their Own Destiny: Group Rights, Gender, and Realistic Rights of Exit', *Ethics*, 112/2 (2002): 205–30.

'Multiculturalism and Feminism: No Simple Question, No Simple Answers', in *Minorities within Minorities: Equality, Rights and Diversity*, ed. Avigail Eisenberg and Jeff Spinner-Halev. Cambridge: Cambridge University Press, 2005: 67–89.

Okin, Susan Moller, with respondents. *Is Multiculturalism Bad for Women?* ed. Joshua Cohen, Matthew Howard and Martha C. Nussbaum. Princeton, NJ: Princeton University Press, 1999.

Parekh, Bhikhu. 'A Varied Moral World', in Susan Moller Okin with respondents, *Is Multiculturalism Bad for Women?* ed. Joshua Cohen, Matthew Howard and Martha C. Nussbaum. Princeton, NJ: Princeton University Press, 1999: 69–75.

Parekh, Bhikhu. *Rethinking Multiculturalism: Cultural Diversity and Political Theory*. Basingstoke: Macmillan, 2000.

Pateman, Carole. *The Sexual Contract*. Cambridge: Polity Press, 1988.

'Self-ownership and Property in the Person', *Journal of Political Philosophy*, 10/1 (2002): 20–53.

Pedwell, Carolyn. *Feminism, Culture and Embodied Practice: The Rhetorics of Practice*. London and New York: Routledge.

Phillips, Anne. *The Politics of Presence: The Political Representation of Gender, Ethnicity and Race*. Oxford and New York: Oxford University Press, 1995.

Multiculturalism without Culture. Princeton, NJ: Princeton University Press, 2007.

Phillips, Anne and Dustin, Moira. 'UK Initiatives on Forced Marriage: Regulation, Exit and Dialogue', *Political Studies*, 52/3 (2004): 531–51.

Phillips, Anne and Saharso, Sawitri (eds.). 'The Rights of Women and the Crisis of Multiculturalism', *Ethnicities*, 8/3 (2008): 291–301.

Poulter, Sebastian. *English Law and Ethnic Minority Customs*. London: Butterworths, 1986.

'The Significance of Ethnic Minority Customs and Traditions in English Criminal Law', *New Community*, 16/1 (1989): 121–8.

Ethnicity, Law and Human Rights: The English Experience. Oxford: Clarendon Press, 1998.

Prokhovnik, Raia. *Rational Woman: A Feminist Critique of Dichotomy*. Manchester: Manchester University Press, 2002.

Puwar, Nirmal. *Space Invaders: Race, Gender and Bodies Out of Place*. Oxford: Berg, 2004.

Railt, Fiona and Zeedyk, Suzanne. *The Implicit Relation of Psychology and Law: Women and Syndrome Evidence*. Philadelphia and London: Routledge, 2000.

Renteln, Alison Dundes. 'A Justification of the Cultural Defense as a Partial Excuse', *California Review of Law and Women's Studies*, 2 (1993): 437–526.

The Cultural Defense. New York and Oxford: Oxford University Press, 2004.

Rowlinson, Matthew. 'Re-Reading Criminal Law: Gendering the Mental Element', in *Feminist Perspectives on Criminal Law*, ed. Donald Nicolson and Lois Bibbings. London: Routledge, 2000: 101–22.

Saharso, Sawitri. 'Female Autonomy and Cultural Imperative: Two Hearts Beating Together', in *Citizenship in Diverse Societies*, ed. Will Kymlicka and Wayne Norman. Oxford: Oxford University Press, 2000: 224–44.

'Feminist Ethics, Autonomy and the Politics of Multiculturalism', *Feminist Theory*, 4/2 (2003): 199–215.

Samad, Yunas and Eade, John. *Community Perceptions of Forced Marriage*. London: Community Liaison Unit, Foreign and Commonwealth Office, 2002.

Sams, Julia P. 'The Availability of the "Cultural Defense" as an Excuse for Criminal Behavior', *Georgia Journal of International and Comparative Law*, 16 (1986): 335–54.

Samuels, Alex. 'Legal Recognition and Protection of Minority Customs in a Plural Society in England', *Anglo-American Law Review*, 10/4 (1981): 241–56.

Schwarzenbach, Sibyl. 'Contractarians and Feminists Debate Prostitution', *Review of Law and Social Change*, 18 (1990–1): 103–30.

Scott, David. 'Culture in Political Theory', *Political Theory*, 31/1 (2003): 92–115.

Scott, Joan. *Only Paradoxes to Offer: French Feminists and the Rights of Man*. Cambridge, MA: Harvard University Press, 1996.

Sen, Amartya. *Commodities and Capabilities*. Amsterdam: North-Holland, 1985.

'Gender Inequality and Theories of Justice', in *Women, Culture and Development: A Study of Human Capabilities*, ed. Martha Nussbaum and Jonathan Glover. Oxford: Clarendon Press, 1995: 259–73.

Shachar, Ayelet. *Multicultural Jurisdictions: Cultural Differences and Women's Rights*. Cambridge and New York: Cambridge University Press, 2001.

'Feminism and Multiculturalism: Mapping the Terrain', in *Multiculturalism and Political Theory*, ed. Anthony Simon Laden and David Owen. Cambridge and New York: Cambridge University Press, 2007: 115–47.

Siddiqui, Hannana. 'The Ties That Bind', *Index on Censorship*, 29/1 (2000): 50–3.

Song, Sarah. *Justice, Gender, and the Politics of Multiculturalism*. Cambridge: Cambridge University Press, 2007.

Southall Black Sisters. *Forced Marriage: An Abuse of Human Rights. One year after 'A Choice by Right'*. London: Southall Black Sisters, 2001.

Spivak, Gayatri Chakravorty. 'Subaltern Studies: Deconstructing Historiography', in *In Other Worlds: Essays in Cultural Politics*, ed. Ranajit Guha and Gayatri Chakravorty Spivak. Oxford: Oxford University Press, 1988: 197–221.

Stoler, Ann Laura. 'On Political and Psychological Essentialisms', *Ethos*, 25/1 (1997): 101–6.

Sunder, Madhavi. 'Cultural Dissent', *Stanford Law Review*, 54 (2001): 495–567.

Sunder Rajan, Rajeswari. *The Scandal of the State: Women, Law and Citizenship in Postcolonial India*. Durham: Duke University Press, 2003.

Sunstein, Cass. 'Preferences and Politics', *Philosophy and Public Affairs*, 20 (1991): 3–34.

Taylor, Charles. 'The Politics of Recognition', in *Multiculturalism and the Politics of Recognition*, ed. Amy Gutmann. Princeton, NJ: Princeton University Press, 1992: 25–74.

Tostan. *Breakthrough in Senegal: The Process that Ended Female Genital Cutting in 31 Villages*. Washington, DC: US Agency for International Development, 1999.

Tully, James. *Strange Multiplicity: Constitutionalism in an Age of Diversity*. Cambridge: Cambridge University Press, 1995.

Turner, Terence. 'Anthropology and Multiculturalism: What is Anthropology that Multiculturalists Should be Mindful of It?' in *Multiculturalism: A Critical Reader*, ed. David Theo Goldberg. Cambridge, MA, and Oxford: Blackwell, 1994: 406–25.

Van Broeck, Jeroen. 'Cultural Defence and Culturally Motivated Crimes', *European Journal of Crime, Criminal Law and Criminal Justice*, 9/1 (2001): 1–31.

Volpp, Leti. '(Mis)identifying Culture: Asian Women and the "Cultural Defense" ', *Harvard Women's Law Journal*, 17 (1994): 57–101.

'Talking "Culture"; Gender, Race, Nation and the Politics of Multicultur-
alism', *Columbia Law Review*, 96/6 (1996): 1573–617.
'Blaming Culture for Bad Behaviour', *Yale Journal of Law and the
Humanities*, 12 (2000): 89–116.
'Feminism and Multiculturalism', *Columbia Law Review*, 101 (2001):
1181–218.
Williams, Raymond. *Culture and Society*. London: Chatto and Windus,
1958.
Wilson, Amrit. 'The Forced Marriage Debate and the British State', *Race
and Class*, 49/1 (2007): 25–38.
Young, Iris Marion. *Justice and the Politics of Difference*. Princeton, NJ:
Princeton University Press, 1990.
'Gender as Seriality: Thinking about Women as a Social Collective', *Signs*,
19/3 (1994): 713–38.
On Female Body Experience: 'Throwing Like a Girl' and Other Essays.
Oxford: Oxford University Press, 2005.

Index

Lightning Source UK Ltd.
Milton Keynes UK
UKOW01f1600070917
308770UK00008B/375/P